Grieve

Stories and Poems about Grief and Loss

Volume 5

HUNTER WRITERS CENTRE

Grieve Volume 5
Hunter Writers Centre
Newcastle NSW 2300

Email: publishing@hunterwriterscentre.org
Website: www.grieveproject.org

Grieve: Stories and Poems about Grief and Loss

22 21 20 19 18   1 2 3 4 5
ISBN-978-0-9954409-6-8(paperback)

Cover design by HWC Publishing
Typesetting by HWC Publishing
2017 Published by Hunter Writers Centre Inc.

© Each short story/poem is copyright of the respective author
© This collection copyright of Hunter Writers Centre

All rights reserved.
No part of this publication may be reproduced, stored in a retrieval system, or transmitted in any form by any means electronic, mechanical, photocopying, recording or otherwise without the prior consent of the publishers.

Table of Contents

Powerless	1
Rachael Mead	
On Saying Goodbye	2
Joel McKerrow	
Deep Breaths and Heartbeats	4
Ky Garvey	
Carpet Beetles	5
Janet Holmes	
Our Small Kingdom	6
Fiona Murphy	
Numbers	8
Kathryn R. Bennett	
I Miss You, Kid	9
Kaylia Payne	
When One Door Closes	10
Josh Wildie	
First Anniversary	12
Laura Jan Shore	
My Truth	13
Cheryl Parker	
The Man in the Mirror	14
Kathy Childs	
Okay	16
Undine Kanowski	
Failed to Provide	18
Ellen Shelley	
Seasons of Grief	19
Vicki Laveau-Harvie	
Scraps	20
Melanie Zolenas-Kennedy	
The Ghost of a Mother	22
Donni Hakanson	

Thirty Years Gone   23
Edwina Shaw

Message to my Mother   24
Gail Hennessy

The Journey   26
Catherine O'Neill

The Sounds of You   28
Sarah Bourne

Ode To My Breasts   29
Katherine Mills

No You   30
Ruth Macaulay

Martin   32
Alison Wheeler

There She Is, My Mother   34
Kathryn Fry

Anna Cries   35
Nicole Melanson

Your Wallet   36
Kim Waters

Last Tuesday   37
Gabrielle Clover

Dear June   38
Sarah Thomson

The Best Moment was also the Worst   40
Erin Vincent

Now She Is Gone   42
Neroli Hay

A Daughter's Funeral   44
Richenda Rudman

Goodbye Sam   45
Carmel Beresford

World's Worst Daughter   46
Jen Loicht

Train Wreck   48
Ken Eastwood

Every Apostrophe	49
Penny Lane	
A Life Lived Free	50
Corinne MacKenzie	
Ordinary Portrait	52
Barry A. Breen	
Making Up	53
David Terelinck	
Saving face (an elegy of sorts)	54
K. A. Nelson	
Missing	55
Heather Warne	
The Grey Goose	56
Nikki McWatters	
Just Me	58
Jo Parker	
Glass	59
Mary Jones	
For Stephanie, Johannesburg 1974	60
Marion Dundon	
Lourdes	62
David Grant Lloyd	
Black on White	63
Bill Bean	
Consummation	64
Vivian Garner	
The Body Mother Made Me	65
Maria Vouis	
All We Have Lost	66
Peter J. Wells	
Design	67
Catherine Wright	
Veteran	68
Anthony Lawrence	
The Breaker Bar	69
Christina M. Aitken	

A Confession — 70
G. Vickers

The Glove — 72
Viktoria Rendes

Whatever Darkness Brings — 73
Kristen Roberts

The Ticket — 74
Vanessa Ives

Meeting Valerie — 76
Adrienne Hunter

Babe — 77
Rob Wallis

Chops — 78
Alexandra Gordon

Focus on the Car — 80
Catherine Moffat

Make-up Lessons — 81
Maya Linden

The Day Before — 82
Janet C. Fraser

My Father Comes to the Island — 83
Renee Pettitt-Schipp

Lay Grievers — 84
Linda Harding

Blue — 86
Verity Laughton

Fragments — 88
Annie Barrett

Numbing the Heart — 90
Miya Dawn

Why — 92
Leith Reid

My Father's Hands — 93
Maree Reedman

Something for Nothing — 94
J.J. Hicks

Position Vacant—Apply Within	96
Jacqui Bakewell	
Grief Riff	98
Mark Tredinnick	
Suddenly You Were Gone	99
Susan Bradley Smith	
Of Cold Hands	100
Justine Poon	
Perseveration	102
Lisa Kenway	
Widows	104
Chris Armstrong	
Ketamine	105
Catherine Johnstone	
Little Man	106
Camille Potgieter	
Three Tiers of Grief	108
Margaret McBride	
Glazier	110
Moya Pacey	
O My Sista	111
Kim Westwood	
I See More Clearly Now	112
Patricia Green	
The Funeral	114
Tim Slade	
Figs	115
Jo Gardiner	
Carrying On	116
Michael T. Schaper	
Hidden Grief	118
Vanessa Yenson	
Hanging On	120
Karen Whitelaw	
Roma alla John: 2011	121
Elizabeth Beaton	

Crank	122
Shelley Booth	
Tick Yes to Donate All Organs	124
Rafael S. W.	
Miss You Much	125
K. Lundman Rocks	
Chronicle	126
Susan Fealy	
A Spill of Unsaids	127
Libby Hart	
Words	128
Nikki McWatters	
Tinkerbell	129
Jessica Kennedy	
Mother as an Art Book	130
Julie Watts	
Saving Sebastian	131
Rose van Son	
The Weight of Words	132
Julia Doig	
Eschatology	134
Sarah Sasson	
Undo Her Fingers	135
Annie Riley	
Inner City Living	136
Wendy McLean	
Old Habits	137
Melissa Willings	
Dear Grief,	138
Kristen Roberts	
Notes on the disappearance of a friend	139
Charlotte Guest	
Virga	143
David Francis	

Bright Shadow	144
Fiona Abbey	
All Souls Are Sleeping	146
Danaë Killian	
A Bridge too Far	148
Tracey Edstein	
The Secret Dreams of Agistment Cattle	150
Philip Neilsen	
The Sword	151
Kim Gunst	
Through the Glucose	152
Bee Penrose	
Overcoming Hurdles	154
Jacqueline Becker	
Not Grief	155
Viktoria Rother	
Indian Summer	156
Ross Gillett	

To spare oneself from grief at all cost can be achieved only at the price of total detachment, which excludes the ability to experience happiness.

- Erich Fromm

Introduction

In the depths of grief have you ever asked 'Why? Why is this so, so painful?' Fromm's words capture one of the many reasons we established the Grieve Writing project – to offer a place for people to express their pain and sorrow and, in doing so, reach others.

It is a joy to find poems and stories by people compelled, by the depth of their loss, to write. We say it is a joy to read these works, which may sound odd, but it's one of the paradoxes of all art, including writing, that we can rejoice in a poem or a painting or a play even as it reveals terrible suffering. It's a mystery, but there is something saving about works born out of such pain.

When we consider how many pieces here show us unrecognised, ignored and avoided grief we know there are many more volumes of Grieve that can be published. This volume is one of many already published and of many to come.

Ross Gillett (poet) and Karen Crofts (Director)
Hunter Writers Centre
Australia
www.grieveproject.org

Powerless
Rachael Mead

Three days without power and the only sounds
are wind, rain and the hiss of flame beneath the kettle.

I don't mind. Quiet is the road blocked by tree-fall,
reminding us that electricity is not the fifth element.

I am reading on the couch when our neighbour
knocks. *Tom has died*, she says.

It's the final erasure of that disease, the one
that eventually steals everything, from his last

conversation to the memory of his wife of 60 years.
She is strong but after she leaves the grey air

seems especially sad and even a little jagged.
The world is not what we want. Our minds,

those tender, playful muscles stiffen and seize,
however hard we work at making ourselves

original. Beyond the glass, the green earth
blurs with rain, the trees bend and crack

in allegories of wind. My heart folds
and folds itself down into a tiny yet infinitely

dense thing: a grain of sand, a mote of dust,
a faraway star we all know full well is dead.

On Saying Goodbye
Joel McKerrow

His words are lost. Silenced by the hum of rotating fan above hospital bed. An incessant buzz. He whispers again, 'Holding hands has never hurt like this.'
    She does not hear.

The fan spins awkwardly and he spins awkwardly—like the shuddering rotator fan, so near to falling, still clinging on. He clings on, to her. Holds her hand like an anchor. His ship is feeling the surge and pull of the rip. The waters have come to cast him adrift.
    'She will not come through this.' He remembers the words, softly spoken by the doctor.
    Doctors always speak too quietly when delivering bad news.
    'What did you say?' he had responded harshly.
    'She . . . We . . . have done all that we can.'

A diagnosis. The finality. The first crashing wave. The tide rose and the ocean came. He chose to ignore it. Ignore the rising water. Stand at the seaside and tell the tide to fall away.

It had not.

He looks down now at his lover. How she shines. She always has. Like early rising sun over the wheat tractor. Every morning. The ploughing and the rising. It had taken this from him too. The sickness. It had taken everything. The last year forced to be in the city for her treatments. City life was a prison and an illness. He could not survive here. 'Melbourne is one person too many,' he'd always say, 'and one tree too few.' Too many and too few.
    He sighs long, leans in, kisses the paper cheek of his wife. Breathes her in. The hospital scent stains her smell and he curses its brevity. Nose on skin and he breathes her deeper. Her rosemary is still there. The oiled wood. The baked bread. Tears well.
    Her eyelids flicker and suddenly they open. For an instant his heart jumps, thinks that maybe she is coming back to him. She smiles. Wrinkled mouth like a petal falling. She holds him in her eyes and then breathes her last.
    The old man breaks. Huge tears rolling down red cheeks. A shuddering sob. He is alone. Torn in two. He gives her one last kiss. Holds

his cheek against hers. The nurse turns off the monitors. He does not notice. This will be the last time he gets to hold her, so he holds her. Like a piece of crumpled parchment. Like a whisper. Like a breath. He holds her. Enfolds his disappearing wife within his roughly hewn shoulders. Presses his piercing emptiness against her and breathes.

He cannot be here any longer.

Though he is really too old to run, he does so regardless. Down empty hospital hall. He hears the nurse call from behind. He cannot turn around. He runs outside, finds the ute, turns the key and he drives. Through the night. He does not stop until he can see it. Home. The farm. He looks to the East. It is morning and the sun is rising over the wheat tractor.

Deep Breaths and Heartbeats
Ky Garvey

I was convinced my heart would stop beating the minute yours did. That I would no longer draw breath once your breath had ceased. I could not exist if you did not exist. Yet, on the day you went away I was caught by surprise. Fate or God or whoever decides the way of these things pointed their cold finger in your direction and your heart stopped dead. Yet my treacherous heart continued to pump blood through my veins. It continued its rhythmic drumming without even missing a beat. Your breath drifted up from your lungs and out through your open mouth and that was that. Prepared to never take a breath again, I expelled all the air from my lungs. But despite my convictions, the air crept in, gradually and deceptively. My chest rose and fell just as it had every day since my birth. I cursed my body for its bloody-minded, mechanical insistence on functioning as bodies were designed to function and its incessant will to live. Did it not know that today was not just any day? Today was the day you went away.

    I wasn't prepared for what you would look like. I'd never seen a dead body before. It was you, yet, not you. Mostly, I remember your eyes: clear, blue, glass marbles. There was no sign of you there, of where you had been. I searched for you in those eyes but you were just a shell with no evidence of your mortal coil.

    The afternoon before you left, I sat beside your hospital bed holding your hand. It was so peaceful there. So quiet. Like there was only you and I left in the world. The phone didn't ring, the nurses were busy with other patients. It was just you and me. You drifted in and out of sleep as I kept my silent vigil. At some point, I inadvertently nodded off, my exhaustion catching me off guard. Together we shared a dreamless sleep. When I awoke, I had managed to climb up next to you in your bed, clutching you as if you would disappear into vapour then and there in my arms. It was our last afternoon together.

    The phone call came at three in the morning. The type of phone call that only ever comes at three in the morning. You were gone. I stood in my lounge room as my body continued to live when yours had chosen not to. It didn't seem possible to be in a world where you no longer existed. Yet my breath continued in and out and my heart had not stopped cold. The clock still ticked, the earth still turned and the sun still shone. The birds did not fall from the sky.

    It's been twenty years of deep breaths and heartbeats and yet I still weep for you as if it was only a moment ago; as if our last afternoon together was only yesterday.

Carpet Beetles
Janet Holmes

Alzheimers is doing to my husband
what carpet beetles are doing
to the deep blue Chinese silk and camel hair heirloom rug
that covers the lounge room floor
they are eating it slowly
invisible themselves
their work obvious in the rough landscape that is now the surface of the carpet
traces of the original design still recognisable in the web background
that is all that is left in some places
in the places they have yet to touch the rich lustre there still
and the overall sense of the carpet in all its former glory sort of intact
it still impresses people who see it for the first time
and if after longer acquaintance they begin to notice the bits which are actually
downright ugly, they are too polite to say so
I love this carpet
I have known it all my life and hope to keep it all my life
but even I know that at this rate it will not out-live me
and that if it races to its demise before I meet mine
I could live without it
perhaps I could have done something to prevent its deterioration
but I had not the means before
and now more worldly wise
I am content enough that it does not last forever
but that's my carpet, not my husband
my husband has been pulled from right under my feet

Our Small Kingdom
Fiona Murphy

I was the youngest of seven. We were twice the size of any other family on the street. We were our own small kingdom.

When Mum passed, a quivering quietness lay over the house. It was as though everyone's voices had dried up. Even the kettle stopped whistling.

I'd stand by the front gate waiting for her mop of curls to crest the hill.

My sureness slipped away as I slept. I'd wake each morning with a thump of a pillow to my head.

'She's done it again!' My sisters would shriek.

After a week of waking up with wringing wet sheets, they kicked me out of the bed. I lay on the wooden floor—skin sticky, eyes stinging.

No one questioned why my bedwetting, unlearnt at five, spontaneously returned four years later.

'Sorry to hear you lost her,' a teacher said to me, hand on my shoulder. She let me beat the chalk dusters together. I hung out the window, the dust settling over my tunic like icing sugar.

Dad grew grim and gritty. He stopped shaving. Grey hairs sprouted on his chin. I missed his voice, the way it'd rumble and rain down on us whenever he told stories. We'd sit slack-jawed; transfixed.

He always managed to weave in things for each of us: a horse for Mary, a car chase for Tom, a boat for Ed, a fortune teller for Charlotte, a ballet dancer for Evelyn, a mechanic for Les, a swordsman for Rupert and a puppy for me. I'd hug Patch whenever Dad mentioned the waggly puppy in the story. Once everyone went to bed, I'd scratch Patch's belly until his eyes would flutter and his long, rough tongue would loll lazily over his sharp teeth.

There are now no more nice stories to tell. Our kingdom was broken.

Our days lost their rhythm. We didn't know what needed to be done. Our hair darkened with grease; long nails tamed only by teeth. The Hills Hoist stood as bare as a winter's tree.

It was up to Evelyn and Mary to go through her wardrobe. I was allowed to sit with my back against the skirting board and watch.

There were three dresses, five slips and a handful of undergarments.

It took us hours. They pressed each dress up against their small slender frames, too shy to put them on. The faded floral cotton hung limply as they hugged them, hems gathering at their bare feet.

Night after night I'd lie on the veranda, eyes on the gate. Waiting. My limbs stayed coiled around myself even though there was no risk of receiving sharp pokes from grumpy sisters. They had grown used to having one less person in bed. They fanned out their hair and let their limbs languish across the mattress.

I'd finally fall into the early stages of sleep; just light enough to listen for the sound of footsteps. I needed her to come back.

Numbers
Kathryn R. Bennett

Fourteen. It's a number that had little significance until now, other than to measure days in a fortnight, days between pays. Now it measures loss. Each fourteenth counts another month since she died. Her husband's birthday, no longer his own occasion, marks six months since his widowhood. With added cruelty, Good Friday and Mother's Day this year share her day of departure. All double doses of grief. All once shared in joy these celebrations are now empty of her vibrant presence.

She was thirty-six when she died. It is much too small a number for death. I count it out as I cut flowers to take to her, and measure its exactness on the odometer as I drive from my home to her grave. It has become a number etched in my subconscious. Frozen in time it will always be her number. I count it as I jiggle my tea bag, the better to deliver the flavour of our shared moments. It's the number of paper cranes we made, her husband and I, and bell tolls we rang as we delivered her garland in Hiroshima. She had visited to celebrate peace. Her death was its antithesis.

Zero is the big empty hole that her absence leaves behind. Daily it threatens to engulf me. 1,905 is the count of her weeks on this earth. The sum of these digits resolves to six, so does her date of birth, so does her date of death. It's the square root of her years lived. Numbers! Why this sudden fascination with numbers? Each one of them multiplies the sense of loss. It emphasises the division between then and now.

And, yet, in their calculation so there is reality, a tangibility of loss. In their size, so, too, there is form.

One is the number of moments I count at a time. My hours and days are singly faced. One day changed my life forever by the actions of one other. One daughter, my only child and my number one best friend. Her one life lived every moment and taken in an instant. One grief is shared by a number too great to count. One community of mourners brought together by her love. One ripple on the water of humanity, her influence radiates into infinity.

Countless are my blessings.
Numberless are my joys.
Myriad are my memories.
Immeasurable is my love.

I Miss You, Kid
Kaylia Payne

What is left of my family is standing outside. A blonde woman dressed in black emerges from the room and nods to us. *He's ready*, she says. My father goes first. My heart starts to beat rapidly as I watch him walk through the doors. He returns five minutes later looking like he has aged five years.

Guys, he was injured. My heart starts beating faster though I don't know why this news comes as a shock. Of course he was injured. He's dead now, isn't he? But his friend, the one who was with him when it happened, said it was internal bleeding. She said he looked fine on the outside. I want to throw up. *There are marks on his face*, Dad says.

Then it is my turn to see him. The casket is on a raised podium at the end of the room—to see inside I have to walk right up to it. I take a step towards him. Then a step back. Then a step forward. Then a step back. I am afraid.

This goes on for too long and other people are waiting for their turn, so I take a deep breath and cross the distance between us, looking down into the casket before I can change my mind. *Just like ripping off a Band-Aid.*

It isn't anything like I'd imagined it would be. I had thought he would look like he was sleeping, his expression peaceful and pure. I had thought it would bring me closure. Whatever the hell that means.

He was injured, I would tell his best friend later during the wake. That is all I say. I don't tell his friend that my brother looked exactly like what he was: a twenty-four-year-old killed in a bad motorcycle accident.

Staring at the bruised and battered corpse, I remember the zombie shows my husband watches. I imagine the body suddenly rising up and lunging at me. Then I feel guilty for imagining that. No one was kinder than my little brother.

I put my hands over his. As I touch them, I am reminded of how much I love him. Even though his hands are cold and waxy and feel nothing like they used to, I remember how much I love him. I realise that the body is my brother. I realise that he really is gone, and I start to cry.

I have so many things I want to say. I want to tell him how special he was. How sweet and funny and clever. How he always made the world seem brighter and better than it is. Instead all I say is: *I miss you, kid.*

I don't tell him that I love him. Even though I did and do. I just say, *I miss you, kid.*

And I walk away.

When One Door Closes
Josh Wildie

Your mum and I never discussed keeping your bedroom door closed. It just happened. I don't even remember who was the last one to shut it. We just both knew we couldn't handle seeing that space. We needed to block it out. Yet when one door closes, it's hard not to look regretfully upon it.

You were smaller than either of us imagined. We knew this would happen but nothing could prepare us for your arrival. Eyes sealed shut. Like in a never-ending dream. The moment so surreal it left us numb.

If this were a movie, we would've left the hospital into a world of dark clouds and torrential rain. Drenched to the bone, we'd collapse into each other's arms and weep. There'd be a sad logic to everything. Our misery would infect the world. Instead, it was a sunny day. People around us chatted. They ordered lunch. Spoke on mobile-phones. Waited for the bus. Held their children's hands. The world carried on. Just another day.

Though you've never been here, our home is filled with your absence. The atmosphere needs to be waded through, leaving us exhausted. Tempers trigger so easily lately. It's no-one's fault but your mum and I blame each other. We still feel love but secretly wonder if it'd be easier if we didn't. If it'd be simpler to just let go. Leave each other behind. Something is always missing. Something we haven't really discussed. Where would we begin?

Our sleep is fitful and uneasy. My dreams always end with the casket door closing with a dull thud. Your face disappearing forever. Until my next nightmare. I think your mum has the same dream. I can't bring myself to ask her.

Last night, while wandering through my insomnia, I stopped before your door. Time crawled until I turned the knob and entered. Your room was as we left it, still awaiting your arrival. I collapsed in the corner and just sat and waited.

Eventually, your Mum entered and sat beside me. We held each other for a while and reminisced about making this room *your* room. How the newspaper-covered floor crunched with each step we took. We'd read yellow was gender neutral but went with aqua. While covered in galaxies of paint specks, we each scanned the room looking for clues as to who you would be. We gazed out your window to see the view you were to grow up with. Each guess about your personality was futile but we couldn't help ourselves. We wanted this room to scream *you*.

Mid-conversation, your mum began to weep into my shoulder. I cried into her hair. We were still there when the sun came up. Another day.

We've left your door open for now. When one door opens, you don't forget all the other doors now closed forever. There's only one thing we're sure of: six months wasn't long enough to know someone as wonderful as you.

First Anniversary
Laura Jan Shore

Outside my window, the you-you-you
of mourning doves and I wake, bewildered.
The redwoods hold each other up,
below the soil, intertwined.

On your side of the bed—I've spread
a felled tree's worth of poetry.
The mulch of memory.

Your stopped breath still
saturates my lungs.
In the night, the moans that startle me
are my own.

Each room where you are not,
your things imprinted with your touch,
I gather into piles to give away or toss.

I carry that spark
my heartwood.
Where do . . . our high-voltage fingers
find each other in the dark?

My Truth
Cheryl Parker

'I am sorry for your loss.'

The echoic phrase hung in the air, well intended, sincere, but of my loss they knew little. Weighted words, naively spoken into my secret world of accumulated grief through the years. The tears burned behind my eyes as the casket morphed into memories of a childhood lost, hiding and being good. The unsolicited fury left its marks on me, often unexpectedly but always with precision and continually covered up. The secret was upheld. My tears told the story people wanted to hear, but the real story was mine and mine alone. Friends filtered past the coffin placing flowers, sentiments of grief visibly expressed with sombre looks and sobbing. I stared. Everything in me wanted to shout the truth but no one would have believed me; the lies had won the day.

The procession finally ceased along with my vague and unrevealing replies. The coffin, containing a significant other, was placed in the car and disappeared down the street. It was over. I looked at my husband and my children. My eldest son sweetly said, 'Don't ever die mum, I didn't like her but look at me, I'm a mess.' I didn't either but I couldn't say it. How do you say it, even to yourself? She was my mother. I felt relief as the burden of unfulfilled expectations, cruel words and actions finally lifted. Yet there was a heaviness in my chest, a disbelief that even at the end she chose to shun me in preference to others who were not kin. The last wound struck with profound accuracy.

The days passed by, the grief soaked up in the festivities of the Christmas season, but the secret grew as her belongings were cleared out. My thoughts became a mixture of unbelief and anger, of questions that would never be answered, of numbness and loss.

The weight of loss built slowly. It took time to work out my tears were ones of lost love and lost opportunity. Never would I have her blessing, love, acceptance for the person I was, a 'sorry', nor her acknowledgement of our truth. I knew I had loved her the best I could. Her brokenness became evident in things I found, the diaries devoid of emotion and the hoarding. My brokenness remained evident in the things I'd longed for: a mother's touch, a listening ear, a welcoming home and true acceptance.

It has been two years. I don't miss her but I long to grieve her absence. I want to know what it is like to be loved and cherished by my mother, for the word 'mum' to hold an alternate truth. Even as I write it feels wrong to express this in its backwardness. I desire the weight of a different loss but my hope of that was buried with her. I love the idea of 'mum'. How do I measure the loss of this idea? I don't think I can.

The Man in the Mirror
Kathy Childs

I call him the man in the mirror as that's where he seems to appear. He started out being quite sociable, laughing at my jokes and generally being around when I felt like a chat but lately he's been overbearing. He followed me into the bathroom yesterday, for God's sake, stood looking in the mirror. We had a chat after that, him and I. Well, I did. I asked him what was going on here and he just stood and looked straight back at me with a quizzical look on his face, like he was waiting for an answer. I'll have to get Margaret onto this. I'll make her a cup of tea before I raise it. She does like a nice cup of tea.

'Who the hell are you?' There's a strange old woman sitting at my kitchen table. 'Are you a friend of Margaret's?' She makes that strange hmmfing sound that Margaret does—perhaps it's catching or maybe hereditary. Maybe she's Margaret's mother or even grandmother—there is a family resemblance. Maybe that's what Maggs will look like when she gets older. We've only been married a few years, Maggs and I. She'll be 27 soon—only a year younger than I am.

I must remember to buy her some flowers. Carnations, I think. They're her favourite. She carried them at our wedding. Or was it roses? How could I not remember that?

The old woman rises stiffly from her chair. She is watching me closely, her eyes are full of pain and I feel a surge of hate for whoever has done this to her.

'Sit down. I'll make you lunch.' She moves around the kitchen, familiar with its layout. It seems she's been here before.

'No need to trouble yourself. I'll wait for Margaret.'

'Suit yourself.' She sits back down, continues drinking her tea.

A thought strikes me. 'Are you with the old guy who's hanging around?'

'Silver hair, blue eyes, confused look?'

'Yes, him.'

'He's my husband.'

'Why are you here?'

'We've been married 56 years.' She ignores my question, keeps talking. 'And now some days I'm a stranger to him.' She has tears in her eyes.

'What's wrong with him?'

'Alzheimer's.'

'Poor chap.' She appears to need something more from me. 'Maybe

I can have a word with him.'

'Maybe you can.' She sips at her tea again. 'But he won't remember.' Tears splash into her tea.

I get up, walk over to the window wondering how I can help.

The lawn outside needs mowing and the garden beds are full of weeds. My mind is foggy. I can't shake the feeling that I'm missing something. Perhaps there is somewhere I'm meant to be. Maybe I'm just hungry. I turn back to the kitchen slowly to avoid twisting my knee and setting off my arthritis.

'Hey, Maggs. What's for lunch?'

I am surprised to see her crying.

Okay

Undine Kanowski

I was twelve years old when my father put his hand through my bedroom window and carved his wrist down to the bone. I'm not sure if he was trying to kill himself but he came very close.

Our neighbours saved him. They heard the crash, ran next door, stymied the bleeding. Thirty more seconds, the paramedics would say later. Thirty more seconds and there would've been no bringing him back.

We heard about the accident the day after it happened. We'd spent the previous night in a caravan park: my mother, my little sisters, me. We spent a lot of transient nights during those years, the worst ones, when the police were frequent visitors to our house.

No one ever explained to me what schizoaffective disorder was. These were words I heard whispered in dark hallways. There was always the air of the clandestine about it, something to be kept hidden, like my family were spies who'd mastered the subtle deception of appearing perfectly normal to the outside world.

I thought my father chose to be crazy; I hated him for it.

I hated him even more when I walked into my childhood bedroom when we finally went home. There was blood on my carpet, blood on my toys, blood on my fairy quilt. Blood on the ceiling, blood on the walls in arcs, blood all over the kitchen where he'd stumbled out to after cutting himself.

I remember being disappointed to find out that he was going to live. I played *Age of Empires* on the computer at home instead of visiting him in the hospital.

He chose this, I told myself. *He chose this*. No one ever tried to convince me otherwise.

When my mother finally decided to leave, no longer able to bear the drinking and hallucinations and the delusions and the time he took a sledgehammer to the wall and brought the whole thing down, I was overjoyed.

No more daily crying. No more daily fear. I let him leak out of my life like poison. I felt free.

A few years later, we found out about his stroke. I was older then. I understood that he'd been sick. I went to visit him to see what was left. When he'd been my father he was tan-skinned and sharp-eyed. Now he was pale and bloated, a shucked shell in the shape of a person. All he could say was, 'Okay.'

'I'm so sorry, Dad.'
'Okay.'
'I forgive you, Dad.'
'Okay.'
'I love you, Dad.'
'Okay.'

I mourn the man he could've been. If he'd received the treatment he needed. If his parents hadn't insisted nothing was wrong. If his illness hadn't been regarded as some shameful personal failure to be kept hidden at all costs.

I grieve for a dead man inside a living body.

But mostly I grieve for myself. Twelve years old, alone in the house playing *Age of Empires* in a room painted bright with my father's blood.

Failed to Provide
Ellen Shelley

They searched for you on my belly

your last watery breath
a breach in the womb
extinguishing your light

I rolled over suffering against the blank hospital wall

condolences arrived in
blue   lavender   white
mingling on the kitchen bench

stemmed soldiers
scented guilt
pity immersed in glass jars

grief sparks such clarity
the spoken and unspoken

your memories would fill a solitary page
a button up pinny   vapour footprints

you were just passing by

in time
web like fascia bind
around striated muscles
absolving our pain

we gathered around you with
prayers   poetry   silence

a shroud of earth
a tiny boxed frame
a nameless man   shovelling you a home

I had failed to provide.

Seasons of Grief
Vicki Laveau-Harvie

outside the hospital beneath a pewter sky
the streets of Paris
heave and yield like lava underfoot

I have flown here
over the molten curve of the earth
to see you

your body jack-knifes on the bed
mutely you fold yourself up
with a view to leaving
your daughters have painted your toenails
an elegant scarlet
and you sweat rivers

I cool the facecloth under the faucet
I hold the straw to your lips
when you swallow you choke

thirteen thousand will die from this August heat
in the cities of France
fragile old butterflies faltering between four walls
while their offspring soak in the simmering sea
off the Spanish coast
and eat pizza with fried eggs on reeking seafronts

you are not old
you will not die now, but later
and not of the weather

your husband will write when they have taken you
his wife, my friend,
to lie beneath snow in the baroque city
of your birth

and far away, I will read his words
heat will sear my scalp
the soles of my feet will burn
I will walk between stone walls that radiate fire

Scraps
Melanie Zolenas-Kennedy

My name is Emily Valcunas. That's like VAL-CHOO-NAS for those of you not up-to-date on your Lithuanian pronunciation. I come from (well, ancestrally) the land of sausage and beetroot if my grandmother's cooking is anything to go by. Or, as my father saw it, the land of warriors and kings. Of Tolkien marshes and strong beer.

Small detail: He'd never actually been there himself.

'Can you believe, Lithuania was once the epicentre of Europe? Dominant!' He frowned, drumming his hands on the steering wheel (at ten and two, thank you very much). 'Well, I suppose we've been getting our backsides kicked for the last four hundred years or so.'

'Five hundred,' I replied, taking a cigarette out of my bag. This was mainly for effect, as the cigarette was bent and crumbling. I'd found it on the footpath the week before and was saving it for such a moment. As I was contemplating the next step (for example, how do you light it?), my father was looking at me like he'd been through this before.

'Give me that,' he said and snatched it away. He jammed it in the side of his mouth. He didn't light it, just chewed on it. 'Don't tell your mother,' he said, eyes on the motorway.

I suppose that's enough of that, because that was eleven months and five days ago. The remainder of a lifetime ago. And my therapist says I need to focus on my own life and what I know to be true and who I want to become. According to Dr. Carly Sattler, I am developing resilience. I am ripping up my old life and turning it into little rainbow coloured scraps.

So thanks for the inspo, Carls. This is for you:

My name is Emily Valchunas but I've already said that. I live in Down Below, a town so tiny and insignificant it doesn't even have its own post office. We drive to the next town over to pick up our credit card bills. I've got two sisters, one older, one younger.

Mum's gone a bit off the rails lately but I've read that's to be expected. I haven't helped things, I guess. She was sobbing over the roast chicken last night so I went and got the bag-that-contains-our-allotment-of-what-once-was-Dad and waved it in her face.

'Dad doesn't like unnecessary emotions!' I screamed.

Then we have my grandmother, Florence, who caught a brown snake yesterday in her kitchen. She wrangled it into a paper grocery sack and stapled the bag shut as proof. You've never seen an angrier snake.

I am slightly concerned that one day this will all be considered normal behaviour for us.

So, I'm trying to write this about me but I'm feeling blank. To be honest with you, I'm feeling really rather un-resilient. Because I'm finding it really hard. I'm feeling like I can't quite talk about who I am without talking about who he was. And that's just that.

The Ghost of a Mother
Donni Hakanson

When he took his life his mother became a ghost.

The gift of life she gave was worthless. Thrown away, discarded; with only a clammy corpse, blotched and defrosting in a funeral parlor, her last goodbye. 'Wake up, this is only a dream' his favourite shirt read. Later, in her hands, a box of ashes that weighed less than half his birth weight and a bill more than twice what the midwife had charged. It didn't seem fair.

Her womb haunted with loss; she wished it had been as barren as her desert heart had become. Spectral and rattling in the ribcage that is her home, with wept futility furrowing a face that might smile in an upturn of lips that rarely reached her eyes. The only place she could scream was where the surf roared and drowned her in its endlessness. An eternity of broken gaped—too many pieces shattered now. Too many pieces lost now. She is only part of a person now, never whole.

Guilt. Without her, he wouldn't have been, would never have existed, this wouldn't have happened. Self-recrimination judge and jury, she finds herself lacking. Terminally. She knew he was troubled; thinking there was more time isn't the same as having it. Why didn't she?

And why didn't he?

Why didn't anyone else?

Regret. So much regret. Hindsight is perfect when one is blind.

The ghost of the mother is a map with no latitude or longitude; a circumference of hollow hopelessness, lost and aimless. The ghost of a mother is a calendar, with birthdays and Christmas, with every full moon, every twenty-third of the month and every cry of a curlew marking pain. The ghost of a mother cries at the baked beans in the grocery store and curls his shirt in the nook beneath her chin, sniffing deeply.

Yet glimmers of wonder emerge. Snippets of joy in angel clouds and rainbows and little birds and feathers and the kindness of others. That dream where he hugged her—and so to keep him in her arms longer she turned it into a waltz and that holding of him danced in her soul, sustaining her a while. Smiles that reach her eyes with a grandchild who cracks her open to let the light in and those who mention his name still. Momentary marvels break the monotony of empty, yet they pass by, becoming touchstones of hope. What lasts is grief and there is no antidote, just a growing around the empty places as time creeps by. It's the aching in her atoms for his presence; the lesson is learning to endure.

After the dark night, each dawn is so bright her heart aches with it, uplifted and painted in crimson. And, so, the ghost of a mother lives the cliché of renewal day by day.

Thirty Years Gone
Edwina Shaw

Thirty years ago, my little brother Matty escaped from the locked ward of a mental hospital and ran through the night to a power line. He took off all his clothes, clambered to the top of the pole and grabbed hold of the buzzing wire with both hands. He was twenty. I was twenty-one.

In a few months, I'll celebrate his fiftieth birthday without him.

In another life he'd probably have children by now, mostly grown. He'd be getting wrinkly with receding hair and a beer belly; wiry hairs growing out of his ears. We'd laugh together about something silly and he'd squeeze the breath out of me in one of his giant bear hugs. Just the way he used to. The same way he hugged me when I saw him for the last time, that long-ago day on a bustling train station in Sydney.

He'd only recently been released from hospital and I was sending him back to our mother in Brisbane. Hugging me so tight I felt my eyeballs bulging, Matty told me he loved me then got into the carriage. When he found his seat he pressed his face against the window, squashing his nose and puffing out his cheeks in a grotesque, funny face because he knew I was about to cry. Three days later he was dead.

Months earlier I'd come home to find him turning blue, another empty bottle of pills beside him. I knew the drill. My mother, siblings and I had been finding him like that a few times every year since his mid-teens. He had schizophrenia. I called the ambulance, rolled him on his side, scooped out the mucous and stayed with him in hospital as his stomach was pumped. But I looked away when he opened his eyes and realised he was still alive. I knew he wished I hadn't found him at all.

On the night he died, I ran out into the darkness and found my way to a playground. On top of the slippery dip, I rested my tear-hot face against the cold metal, remembering our childhood adventures, and I roared at the sky. But mixed in with my grief was a feeling of relief. Relief that my soft-hearted, incredibly brave brother was no longer suffering. That I didn't have to witness his pain any longer. For many years I felt guilty about that sense of relief mingling with my grief. But now I know he must have felt it too. And that it's all right.

Thirty years gone. Perhaps my grief has faded a little but on days like today it feels as hard and ugly as ever and all I want is Matty back the way he was before schizophrenia took him. To ride bikes down rocky gullies together and swim in waterholes. To burn sausages over secret campfires in the backyard. To see him laugh with his whole heart. To be squeezed in his arms until he takes my breath away.

Message to my Mother
Gail Hennessy

in the kitchen of my childhood
incandescent coal glows
in the womb of the fuel stove

my nine year old self
reaches to your collar bone

you tell me
'I have been to see the doctor
he cannot hear a heartbeat'

did I speak then of angels
urge you to baptise the baby
as soon as she is born

we've already named her Margaret.

I hope I didn't mention Limbo
for I had learnt my catechism
and you a mere convert to the faith

I remember leaning a little way down
to press my ear against your belly
straining to hear a metronome's tick

is that how a heart beats?

I believed I could bargain with God
in the power of prayer

in miracles that could reverse mortality
deliver you a daughter and me a sister

What solace would I offer now
confronted with that verdict

would I repeat words I've heard
that baby was not meant to live

God has taken it to spare you suffering
there are no words I could have said
to assuage your grief

you took my child's trust and let
me dream the nine months through.

The Journey
Catherine O'Neill

I found out I was pregnant the same day my Dad learnt he was dying. He was given three months to live. He lasted eight. In the months that followed, I wondered at the similarities between the birthing and dying process. We both became fatigued, struggled to eat and experienced nausea. We suffered pain, although mine was nothing compared to Dad's. We both experienced the normal anxieties and fears people face in our situation but Dad had more than me to face. We were overwhelmed with the care and support received from those around us.

Our journeys continued together, every week Dad became more frail and thinner whilst my baby grew bigger and stronger. Dad weighed forty kilograms at his death. I was sure I found every kilo he had lost. After seven months of palliative care, Dad was admitted to hospital. Unexpectedly, I was hospitalised two days later. My baby was at risk and I was induced that very day. Being premature, my baby remained hospitalised in the city, several hours away from home. Having been with my Dad every day of his battle, I could no longer be at his side. I grieved at a loss that had not yet occurred.

Time passed and finally I could take my baby home to meet Dad. By then his eyesight had failed, he was too weak to hold my baby and, in his confusion, he did not want the baby close in case he caught his cancer. It broke my heart that my Dad who had longed for a grandson would not share in the life of this beautiful little boy. I think it broke my Dad's heart too and he died not long after. That night, before he slipped into unconsciousness, he said to me, 'I love you, Flossy.' Those were his last words.

I remember the florist delivering sympathy flowers and congratulation balloons to me on the same day. She looked confused and asked if this was correct. I confirmed it was. She flippantly said, 'you are having a bad day, aren't you?' Yes, I was.

The first time anyone saw my son was at Dad's funeral. My baby's first mass was for his Grandpa, his second was his own baptism a week later. At both we celebrated life. At both I cried.

Life and death were so closely entwined during my pregnancy. Grief is tough. Grief whilst caring and loving a newborn is tougher. There is no space for grief, no chance to sit and cry, to mourn and remember. Now, as my 6 month old rolls across the floor at my feet, I look back on all that occurred. Dad's memorial cards and the baby thankyou letters have all been posted. My life continues in a new direction. I miss Dad every day. My grief, not properly processed, is never far away. Both my husband and I have green eyes. My baby has striking blue ones. Dad's were blue as well. The journey continues.

The Sounds of You

Sarah Bourne

I was half asleep on the sofa when you came in, the dog curled at my feet, the cat against my stomach, leeching my warmth. I knew it was you without opening my eyes by the sounds you made. The squeak of the shoe that you always meant to take to Mr Minit to get fixed, the swish of your jacket as you shrugged it off and hung it over the chair. I felt the faintest of breezes on my cheek as the air eddied around your movements in the otherwise still room.

You were careful not to wake me, and I smiled to myself at your consideration. But then the dog lifted her head, and the cat stretched and resettled. Putting your bag down you stepped lightly. Your footfall as you approached was as familiar to me as my heartbeat. The rhythm of your breath could have been my own. Your lips brushed my forehead and your hand, as you stroked my hair, was as light as a ray of moonlight.

I reached out my hand and you took it, lifting it to your lips for a kiss.

You went into the kitchen and I heard you pour yourself some water, take ice out of the freezer and drop it, crackling, into the glass. I heard you sink into a chair and sigh, letting go of your day, relaxing into home.

'I'll start dinner soon,' I called.

'No hurry,' you said.

I heard the creak of the stairs as you went up to change out of your suit, and your footsteps overhead in the bedroom, moving from door to wardrobe to chair, where you would have sat to take off your shoes, back to the door and down the stairs again, the third one from the bottom, the one that needs replacing, groaning under your weight.

'Just going to water the garden,' you said, and the back door clicked shut.

Had I known it was the last time you would ever come in, I would have opened my eyes to you. I would have told you how much I love you for laughing at my awful jokes, and for not judging me when I cry at old movies. I would have said that you create meaning and light in my life and that when you're around everything makes sense.

I would have feasted on your face, gorged on the softness of your gaze, the tenderness in your eyes. I would have run my hands over your body and made a cast of you in my mind. I would have seared the memory of you into my soul.

Instead, I listened to the sounds of you, and I listen for them still in the silence of our home.

Ode To My Breasts
Katherine Mills

The weight of my loss
Is the contents of a B cup bra.
Both of my breasts were removed.
Amputated.
Nipples, tissue – all of it
Gone.
Replaced with muscle cut from my back
And silicone gel implants.
C cup. Why not?
I will forever mourn the loss of my breasts
A symbol of femininity
Synonymous with my sexuality.
All sensation – lost
I will never again feel the joy
Of a caress, a nibble, a nudge.
Synonymous with the maternal.
All ability to breast feed – lost
I am left with permanently perky breasts
Hot and sweaty in summer
Icicles in winter.
A forever nagging back ache.
My upper body is a patchwork quilt of scars.
A constant reminder of my battle with cancer.
A battle – fought and won
A battle that will never leave me
A battle I will always fear is not my last . . .
Farewell to my beautiful
But deadly breasts.

No You
Ruth Macaulay

There was no casket. There were no weeping relatives in black, no hard pews, no renditions of *Amazing Grace* by your cousin. There was no eulogy. There was no goodbye. No one came to the wake and ate spinach and ricotta puffs and shared merlot and memories because there was no wake. There is no headstone. No epitaph. There is nothing left in this world to acknowledge that, briefly, you were here.

Do you see me sitting in that cold blue bathroom, counting every second, holding my breath? Desperate to look down but, no, it won't be accurate until two minutes is up. And, look, there are two tiny lines! You see them, don't you? Materialised on that little white stick, holding pee and promises. I cried that day too. I've cried every day since.

Your dad called you Smush. Little Smush. See him rubbing his face on my belly, giving you your first kisses? Little Smush. You were smaller than a pin point but you were so there, so real. Can you see us drinking Earl Grey by the orange glow of the heater, playing footsies with socked feet and dreaming of who you might be? We would flick through Domain looking for a house with more than one bedroom. We would see prams in shops and kids on playgrounds and smile to each other, sharing our delicious secret.

And, look now, can you see me? Again in the cold, blue bathroom, again, looking down, this time seeing red. And can you hear it? The sobbing, the calling out to your dad, his footsteps as he runs from the kitchen. Watch us drive to the hospital, fingers crossed, desperately hoping. This can happen sometimes, can't it? This is normal, right?

The doctor gave me a pat on the arm and a pamphlet. Can you read the print on the front in gaudy orange letters? *Coping With a Miscarriage —What to Expect.* It went straight into the recycling with the lawnmower catalogues and the empty Cornflakes box. Do you see us on that same couch, hugging away the night? Do you see me in that same bathroom, in a foetal position on the floor, the tiles pressing patterns into my cheek?

There were balloons. There were cards. There were tears and embraces and gluten-free casseroles left by neighbours. There were nights where I drowned in salty sobs and wine. Nights where I ate a whole pot of mashed potato to myself. Nights where I ate nothing at all. There was fury, screaming, guilt, shame, mascara stains on my good cotton pillowcases. There were times when I wondered if it was my body to blame or karma or divine intervention or natural selection or just pure random cosmic chance. There were grief counsellors and group sessions and kind words and mental health plans. There was everything we could possibly need.

But there was no you.

Martin
Alison Wheeler

He wakes every half hour and sits bolt upright.

I spring from where I am lying on the floor. My Mother, close by, sleeps uneasily in a chair.

He stares at me, his skinny shoulders heaving with the effort to breathe.

'What's wrong, Martin? What do you need? You're tired aren't you?'

His eyes search my face.

'Exhausted,' he whispers.

'Will I massage your feet?' I ask.

He nods.

I kneel and gently massage them.

He doesn't want to lie down but the effort to sit becomes too much. He tries to lower himself to the bed. He is too weak, though, and collapses like a toy.

I lie down again, annoyed that Mum's fitful sleeping makes it hard for me to hear my brother breathe.

Silence.

The light goes on. Martin bolts upright again.

His hollow eyes stare into my soul.

I sit next to him on the bed; his head rests on mine.

I have to protect him, help him make it through the night. Tomorrow will be better.

'Martin . . . lie down . . . why don't you hand it over to me? . . . I'll look after you.'

These words seem to soothe him.

He can't fight anymore.

He lies down and reluctantly closes his eyes.

This is the last time Martin sits up.

Tomorrow he will be dead.

I am woken by someone telling me 'it's time'.

We stand around Martin's bed.

We watch his chest rise and fall.

Each time the gaps between his breaths get longer but he manages to find air somewhere in the room and drag it into his lungs.

We wait.

But he doesn't breathe out again.

I touch his hand, put my ear up to his face, put a hand on his chest.

I look to the nurse and she nods.

I don't understand. This is my big brother Martin. An awesome guitarist, a talented surfer, the funniest guy in the room. Where has he gone? Why isn't he still here with us?

My Mother lets out a primal, guttural moan from the deepest part of her being.

We sit in the living room. Nobody talks. There is nothing to say.

We meet the funeral people. Mum picks out a white coffin and says the child is not supposed to die before the parent.

We sleepwalk though the funeral. I cry at the faces of Martin's friends.

I never hear my mother cry again about Martin's death. Each Christmas she suffers excruciating chest pain and is raced off to hospital. Tests are done but nothing is ever found. She knows it's grief but there is nothing she can do about it. How is a mother supposed to 'deal' with losing her only son to a long, drawn out, painful death? Her heart reminds her every year.

I don't know where Martin has gone but I still find myself talking to him. I ask if he's all right and he says he's okay and I should chill out. I say goodbye. Life goes on.

There She Is, My Mother
Kathryn Fry

I'm looking for penguins in limestone holes
below the heath—gums, geebungs, grasses
picture-perfect in the salty wind—the waning
moon setting. Out of nowhere a fantail turns
and twists his feathers. And there she is,

walking as ever down the hall, her cool cotton
dress (floral waist-band and hem); hair fluffed,
face powder-fresh after every afternoon shower.
But here I've upset these masked lapwings
into a cackle of code over Nepean Bay.

Hers were Tiffany's dreams at breakfast,
a catwalk on Fifth Avenue, the fall of crepe,
the cut of linen, always the choice of colour.

She'd be the purple crowned lorikeet, flighty,
bright as every crayon in the pack, chalking up
the crimson of these flashy myrtle flowers.
But give her strelitzia's gold or gerberas, bowls
of pink magnolias, camellias large as plates.

Alone in those final years, she broke bread
for the butcherbird at her kitchen window.

A long time gone, you said. But I find you
in my sister's voice, my thinning hands
and now even where you've never been.

Anna Cries
Nicole Melanson

Anna cries on the other side of the door,
crouching over porcelain,

her almost-child a watercolor
dissolving towards the sea.

She cries for me
but will not let me in.

Her sobbing tessellates
in waves across the floor.

She cries names I do not recognize
and then, for God,

whom I would beg to pluck her up
and knot her back together

if only He would hear
Anna crying on the other side of the door,

a nest of hair gathering
the small birds of her hands.

Your Wallet
Kim Waters

It came to me after you'd gone
Oblong, hand-stitched and empty,
Life flattened out of its pockets.

I kept it in a carved wooden box
With a two dollar note and
A photo taken just before you died

At thirty-four years of age.
Sometimes I'd open it out
Inhale your long ago scent.

One summer day, my fingertip,
Tinged with baby oil, left a smear
On its perfect tanned surface.

It was never the same,
Time overtaking memory,
The present tattooed on the past.

Last Tuesday
Gabrielle Clover

Last Tuesday I went searching
deep in the bones of the house

buried in suitcase coffins, closed in albums, tethered to photographs – memories
1986 – the plastic pages clung to each other – Christmas at Kiama
I gave you a rock with eyes painted on
you gave me a shell, held it to my ear
told me the ocean echoes the closest heartbeat

but the tides of adolescence caught you by the ankle and dragged you out to sea
you didn't leave a note
so all I have are the shards of our last conversation, edges sharp with regret
if I had known that the dial tone of the phone
would become the flatline of your heart
I would have talked forever

I would have told you
you are not alone, tossed about by the whitewash of life
where living and drowning both feel the same
I would have drained the ocean – so you could catch your breath
I would have told you
that there would be a day where the ice of depression would thaw
the world would turn from dish water grey
to the dancing Aurora Australis
if you could just hold on
but you couldn't
and we were sentenced to a lifetime of missing you

Last Tuesday I went searching
deep in the bones of the house

I found you there
in a polystyrene box – ashes lighter than life
I took you back to the ocean to play once more
in the amniotic fluid of our childhood shore
I opened the lid – the breeze breathed over you and you flew free
I put a shell to my ear
I could hear your heartbeat

Dear June
Sarah Thomson

Dear June,

I'm sitting here at my desk, watching as the first coat-wrapped figures begin to crawl over the cobblestones below. I seem to have lost all sense of time and routine. Dawn is cracking and swallowing me up in its widening jaws. The wooden pen you gave me twirls uselessly in my fingers—my gnarled, old fingers with their veins now on the wrong side of the surface. Dawn is cracking and I am snatching at the gossamer of inspiration. But the wind is blowing outside and it just drifts higher.

Simpkin got in a terrible state yesterday because I slept past his breakfast time again. I woke to him pacing the pillows around my head, meowing his little lungs out. I wanted to say, 'I am worn to a ravelling, Simpkin. There's no more twist,' put on my nightcap and turn away like the old Tailor of Gloucester. But our Simpkin has all the petulance of Beatrix Potter's incarnation without, I suspect, the moral consciousness to temper it. I can tell he, too, is having trouble adjusting to your absence. He still curls up in his old spot at the foot of the bed, in the gap between our feet, though half the mattress is free now.

Ah, June—I have become aware lately of the loneliness which is sharpening the edge of my grief. A cat is all very well but his limitations must be admitted when it comes to the finer points of conversation.

I thought I could get through life with only you and my smattering of old friends. I was not prepared for old age; I was not prepared for my loved ones to start wilting and falling like winter flowers around me.

We were fools to think we needed no one but each other—rather, I am the fool, proven by fate. Had you been the one to sit at this solitary desk it would have been you but it would have upset the balance of nature too much had I turned out to be the wiser of us. I should have known it would always be me left to walk this road alone, at the end.

We always told each other we did not regret our decision against having children. And, believe me, I never did feel the need for anything more in my life than you by my side every morning. Yet I have become aware, since you've been gone, of an absence which I think was always inside me, lying dormant. A dull ache at the back of my mind which has migrated into my chest and risen to a singing frequency like tinnitus. Or perhaps it is you who abides in that pain: a memory aid.

But look at me rambling away when I should be working. I will write again soon; talking with you always helped to clear my mind and I'm afraid I've become too reliant on the process to give it up now.

Always yours,
Howard.

The Best Moment was also the Worst

Erin Vincent

I don't know where I was when they died. I could have been out shopping at Babies R Us, sitting down to dinner with my husband or painting their room.

To think they might have been taking their last 'breath' while I was laughing at The Simpsons; that as I watched Brian put the Ikea cots together their little hearts were slowing down. To think that the kicking stopped long before I noticed.

I gave birth to Sam at 21 weeks. He was stillborn. I gave birth to John a few hours earlier, though I was told he died much earlier in the pregnancy.

At first I felt an overwhelming guilt that I'd killed my children. That something I did caused their deaths. From the glass of wine I had before I knew I was pregnant to my time in the military, thinking I'd exposed them to something deadly.

Then came the sickness. Trips to the emergency room, the cardiologist, and the urologist found nothing.

It was grief, of course, but how was I to know grief had physical symptoms? They don't show you that in the movies or on TV. People learn such terrible things from the movies, things that are detached from reality. It's like grief propaganda, teaching people how they should be. As a result people say the coldest things. I was told I should have had an abortion, that I should get pregnant again right away, that I should be on meds so I don't have to grieve.

But, oh, how I grieve. I stare at the living room wall for hours. I scream at the showerhead. I don't want to leave the house. I wish the worst on happy people. I'm jealous of other mothers. I'm angry that no one acknowledges me as a mother. I think I'm a murderer.

It's all so contradictory. I never thought that I could be so in love with someone who I never really knew and yet be so tormented as a grieving parent for those whom I have always known—my children.

Oh, how naïve I was as to the intensity of the love one can have for a stillborn child. I have since learned that the bond I have with them is unbreakable despite the fact that they came into this world already dead.

Oh, how furious I feel when I think of how their age seems proportionate to how the world views their worth. My own grandmother said I shouldn't be so sad because, 'they were only infants, after all.' I've even heard stories of people telling parents of stillborn children that they are not real parents.

You know, I thought I might die of a broken heart. But the problem with a broken heart is, it doesn't come up on any scans, in any x-rays, in any tests. A broken heart keeps beating even when you wish it wouldn't.

Now She Is Gone
Neroli Hay

My sister was due to leave for the train and she didn't want to go. I asked her to join me for one or two days in the mountains. In the end, she stayed for four.

'It doesn't matter if I miss the train,' she said. 'I can always catch the next one,' and she plonked herself down on the couch and picked up a magazine.

I stood in the doorway and stared at her. I had looked forward to this retreat for months.

'But it does matter,' I screamed inside my head. 'I need time to rest and be on my own right now. Go now. I need you to go.'

I knew she was dying but didn't know when. Her struggle had been going on for years and the end would come as would the mist and rain.

We sat on the balcony gazing through the trees, trying to make sense of our days of living. In the evening, she chattered inconsequential things and called me to watch television commercials with her, with the sound of the TV turned up blaring. And I wrapped myself in a coat and walked outside and asked God to help me, just help me; give her what she needs.

In the morning, sun streamed into our living room and she sat bare to the waist while I massaged her back, stroking the pale, thin skin with my fingertips, trying to remove toxins from her body that no longer had lymph glands to do the work.

'How long can she last?' I wondered. 'How long will I feel this ache?' I would have done anything to stop the pain.

'If the cancer comes back, I won't have any more treatment,' she said. 'I haven't told anyone but I want you to know.' There was a pause while the words sank in but my fingers kept stroking.

'I'm glad you've decided,' I said, 'because you've had enough,' and knew I was speaking for both of us.

'Perhaps death won't be that bad,' I continued, 'just a brief passing over.' There was a pause again. Were my words too cruel? Was I again too hasty?

She mustered up the energy to go home at last and I bundled her onto the train. As the carriage pulled away and her face began to fade I tried to imprint the essence of her deep inside my memory.

The cancer came back and she had more treatment, but, after more years, death finally claimed her ravaged body and she passed away.

At first, I was relieved she was gone. The endless chatter had ended, the doctors' appointments and cycles of painful treatment. Yet after I had sipped tea in the well of stillness for a while, I couldn't believe how much I really missed her.

    She is gone and how I wish I could hold her to me! But there is nothing I would have said or done to try and make her stay.

A Daughter's Funeral
Richenda Rudman

Words stop and start
From friends corked with sadness,
Turning a rack of agony
In small tight increments
And the weeping, weeping
Mother's wolf cry
Purging the forecast future
And holding the past like pearls.

And the flowers, oh, the flowers
In fierce coloured coats
Bursting with every lost sunrise and sunset
And scents of a newborn,
Fires in winter,
Exotica.

They're flaming, grasping the coffin
Virgin, shiny-white
Led by a grey-suited woman
Stitched with a company logo
And a voice five minutes from
The supermarket price check,
Telling us to leave row by row
And make room for the dead daughter.

Goodbye Sam
Carmel Beresford

As we walked along a passageway the doctor turned to me and said, 'Your son is going to die tonight.'

I was angry. 'How does he know?' I thought, 'He's not God!' Sam was fading away and there was little more that could be done for him.

We were taken to him. I sat as close as I could to Sam and held his hand in mine. By now, tears were streaming down my face.

I kissed Sam's hand and wiped my tears with it. I leaned down so that my mouth was beside his ear. I spoke so only he would hear. I told Sam I loved him with all my heart and that I didn't want him to die. My tears were for the sadness I was feeling because he was leaving me. I told Sam my voice was the first voice he heard when he came into this world and I wanted mine to be the last he heard as he left it. I was in a state of despair but I did not want to be consoled by anyone. I continued whispering my thoughts to Sam. Then I sensed quietness around me. When the doctor saw me look up, he moved around to the other side of Sam's bed, reached up and turned off the monitor. Sam was gone. I again leaned to his ear and quietly said, 'You go now, Sam, with all the love I have in me. I don't know what I will do without you.' I kissed his cheek, slowly stood up and moved away. I couldn't speak. We were taken to a small room and left alone for a few minutes.

In a cruel twist, Sam had to be officially identified. We had sat by my son's bed for eight days watching him slowly dying and now he needed to be identified? I was angry that Sam was dead and I needed to leave that room. I desperately wanted to go back and sit with him forever. I wanted to hold him and not let him go.

I walked up beside Sam's face and looked down. I was heartbroken. The doctor said, 'Is this your son, Samuel John Beresford?'

I simply answered, 'Yes.'

The doctor walked away. He had what he needed.

The respirator tube had been removed from Sam's mouth and his lips had turned blue. I was distraught seeing this; the process of death had begun. I reached out and caressed his cheek. Up and down my hand went, drawing closer to the corner of his mouth. I followed the shape of his lips, wanting desperately to warm them again and change their colour back to pink. I stood there following the outline again and again and, then, for the last time, I leaned over to his face. I kissed his cheek. I kissed his cold lips.

I quietly said, 'Goodbye, my son, goodbye.' It was a moment between just the two of us—a mother and her son.

World's Worst Daughter
Jen Loicht

On a crisp June morning a year to the day after my mother died, I drove to her house with trepidation.

Mum's last few months hadn't been good and not just because of her illness. The tension in our relationship, always fraught, had inexplicably escalated as her health declined despite my best intentions to be more patient, accepting. Differences of opinion had erupted, as ever, into massive arguments—but now she was so sick, our volatile co-existence seemed more dysfunctional than usual. I still morphed from forty-something woman into teen tantrum-thrower when in her presence, though I longed to reinvent myself as a saintly type who would be warm and loving no matter how frustrated I got. But, try as I might, the sad truth was that not even after a terminal diagnosis could I love my Mum without condition. Maybe only a mother, which I wasn't, was capable of that kind of love.

Just what had I expected from her as she neared the end of life? Perhaps that she would grab it and enjoy every day that remained, stop her habitual and useless worrying once and for all, be in the moment, write a 'bucket list'. But such modern notions had meant little to Mum. I, meanwhile, had adopted them with gusto and persisted in trying to sell them to an utterly disinterested customer, my mother, because she was so bereft I couldn't bear it. I'd also tried to prise her open to the idea of alternative medicine. After all, we had been assured that surgery, chemo and radiation would never cure her. In fact they just made her sicker, frailer, unhappier. Yet she threw herself at them again and again while I begged her to try something different, kinder, less rough on her poor, depleted body. On and on we had fought, a sad battle with no winners.

I reached the driveway of her home, which was now mine, and steeled myself for the desolation that would soon, surely, overwhelm me. Not to mention the guilt. I didn't deserve this house, I was a bitch. An ancient memory made me cringe as it came into focus: a young me yelling 'I hate you!' after a particularly bad disagreement; Mum replying simply that she loved me anyway.

I didn't want this house, wanted her to still be living here—canoodling with her man, laughing at sitcoms, cooking Austrian food. I didn't miss our endless talking, tears and misunderstandings, but missed knowing she shared this planet with me. I missed indulging in iced coffees together—our favourite drink, some common ground. I missed holding her, silently, when she'd been scared of the unknown. It seemed to calm her, made me feel useful for a change.

The moment came to enter the empty house. If there was ever a time I could have used a sibling . . . I turned her key, stepped inside and waited to feel hopeless, shitty, alone. Instead, I was enveloped by love.

Train Wreck
Ken Eastwood

I was watching him near the doorway of the crowded train. Red baseball cap; just enough groomed facial hair and a smile he obviously considered cute.

When she walked in there wouldn't have been a red-blooded male in the carriage foyer who wouldn't have noticed. She squeezed past him and ascended the stairs, leaning at the top, her short skirt giving us all a view to the moon and back. I glanced. Yeah, even in my dark mood I glanced.

But this guy, this arrogant little prick, just stood there, mouth almost drooling, just openly staring at her. I watched him with increasing distaste. He kept trying to catch her eye and finally she looked down at him and he gave her a well-practised half wink and his best smile.

I glanced back at her. Those legs. Those legs. Maybe I once gawked as greedily at my wife. Teenage sweethearts. When everything was full of promise and life and hope and dreams and passion. When sex was unstoppable and desire unquenchable and love, whatever that is, would last forever.

My fourth finger still feels weird. I hadn't realised until I took off my ring that I used to regularly flick it with my thumb, subconsciously checking it during the day. Now I'm jolted back as my thumb finds only skin. Finds part of me missing, perhaps.

Terri asked the other day how I feel about being 'on the market' again. Am I? Is that what this is? Competing with cocky young arseholes with practised winks on crowded trains? Oh yeah, great catch I am. Two kids, wrong side of 40, living in a rental.

Yet I chose this, didn't I? Me, the one who supposedly had everything, chose to end it. To walk away from a bloody mess that was incapable of being resuscitated, like some heartless triage at a train wreck.

When I first used the D word in regards to us, I plunged into black. It's such an awful word. It has no nuance, no subtlety of meaning, no context. You can separate eggs or separate the sheep from the goats. But divorce only means one, ugly thing. It's as singular in definition as isthmus or marzipan. Yet it whispers failure. And death. Of something that was but is now snuffed out like a cigarette butt under a boot.

I chose freedom, certainly. But the final, signed papers in my backpack today don't feel like a ticket to ride. They weigh me down like a death certificate.

Every Apostrophe
Penny Lane

There are wounded hours   when
every apostrophe reminds me of me

when I cannot release my stare
from the shape of those punctuations
every fat black dot   my head-swell of grief
every tail   the foetal curl of me cradling empty space

when I cannot retrieve my focus on their intent
signs of belonging yet   signs of something missing

some one missing   my child
you were and now aren't   could and now can't

Seeking refuge in books
I encounter those foetal curls and   not only those
every comma is a tumbled apostrophe
giving me pause for thoughts of me

I shelve the books   unfold the maps
for geography omits most apostrophes
Hawks Nest   where pitching the tent I remember
your laughter in the muffle of canvas   and after
on Bennetts Beach your flailing run down the tufted sand dunes
and all along Jimmys Beach kicking and scooping lapping water
scattering seagulls   the gawky awkwardness of you
tripping tumbling on a tent peg   I remember

I lose myself in places I have been with you

You curl like an apostrophe on the blank sheet of me
someone missing   yet someone belonging still

A Life Lived Free
Corinne MacKenzie

I gaze at the photo in my hand. My sister's long red hair flies in the wind, auburn tresses streaming back from a smiling face. She gazes into the distance, out to sea.

My sister's first boat was called *Freedom*.

This is how I like to remember her. Not in the hospital bed, tubes running from her arm and mouth—connections to a machine with numbers and lines that measure heart rate, blood pressure and breaths per minute.

I watch my sister's hand reach towards the tube down her throat. But a sling holds her arm back, restricting her reach, so she can't pull out this source of irritation. It is vital so it must stay in, for now at least, while the doctors run tests to understand what's happening inside.

We take turns holding her hand. I'm unsure what she knows or even if she knows we are here. Can she feel it when I gently squeeze her hand? Her fingers do not return the pressure. Her hand rests warm but strangely heavy and unresponsive in mine.

I imagine her in the dark. Or is there no sensation of light and dark at all? Does she hear us talk as we keep vigil by her hospital bed? Does she lie alone behind this tumour that's invaded her brain unable to communicate and make her thoughts known? Is she listening? Hoping she'll be back with us soon? The machine beside her registers vital signs.

The doctors take us aside to explain the results.

When the nurses tell her they are removing the tube, her tears start flowing, filling her eyelashes, thick and wet, until overloaded droplets fall onto her cheeks. I use a tissue to wipe them but they keep refilling her lashes and spilling onto her cheeks, sliding downwards in a constant trickle. That's when I'm sure that she can hear and she understands what this means.

The day she died a single red rose was delivered to each of her family and godchildren—her final message, 'A rose, a symbol of my love'.

I recall her telling me how one night she and her husband sat on the deck of their yacht in the Whitsunday Passage. They drifted under a near full moon. And on this night a family of whales came by, inquisitive, up close to the boat. The massive bulk of one came up first from the depths to loll in the waters beside them, churning gleaming splinters of glowing phosphorescence and foam in the moonlit sea. Its great grey head and body surfaced causing a swell of gently rocking waves. One eye looked up, a mysterious primal gaze directed towards the boat, seeming fixed on her. And she felt, she knows it sounds silly, but it felt like they knew, and they were here for her—so long they stayed, and with their young too, communing through the night.

I like to imagine her still sailing and free.

Ordinary Portrait
Barry A. Breen

"Something like living occurs"
         – John Ashbery

He was so ordinary as to be
a miracle. He drank a little too much, earned
usually not enough and never missed Mass.
He smoked a pipe, jigged to the rhythm
of Irish music but was tone deaf – cribbage
and euchre were the tunes he grew up on –
he was tallish and handsome in a house
full of tall, handsome men. Later
my mother massaged his scalp every day
to strengthen his hair. He worked
as best he could through the Depression
away from home selling insurance to skint
and skinflint Catholics in the district where
his grandfather had settled and his father
had lost the farm. In the war he served
in the army, away again, with a wife
and three children at home and two more
to come when it was all over. Of the war
he remembered one almighty thunderstorm
and a huge goanna running across his bare
feet in Darwin. He came home and ran
a pub. He ran another. He kept a shop
where I learned to charleston to Sweet
Georgia Brown, leaning on the counter after
school waiting for customers. Then he went back
to selling insurance only now he was called
an assurance representative. Some said
he was proud, that he loved an argument;
a good debate he would have said. Where
the parish went politically, he went too.
His sons did not necessarily follow.
He died in his early sixties, far too young,
like all the big handsome men of his family,
the smokers and drinkers. There was abruptly
a huge gap then where this ordinary man
had been. That might have been the miracle.

Making Up
David Terelinck

Your highlights perfect;
just the right amount of blush
to hide a blemish I never
thought unsightly. Mother's
marcasite clip glimmers
in the empathy of recessed
lighting. Small pyrite chips
police your hair, restraining
that plush mane which combusts
with the slightest draught of wind.

Suddenly I'm breathless,
winnowed by the bloom
of high cheek bones. My fingers,
deliberate with memory, schlep
these alpine summits once again.
I take your hand, admire
the artistry of polished
nails. The careless would miss
the finest needlework
that closed the vein you opened.

Bring me the make-up artist
who can white-wash tears
away. One who will undertake
to sedate my "what-if" mind.
It's not enough to stop time
in your face and hands. Send
the watchmaker who can
reset life – just enough –
that remorse and grief
have no business being here.

Saving face (an elegy of sorts)
K. A. Nelson

His burial was a private,
grave-side service. She went
like an Egyptian Queen
      with her trappings:

Ezibuy catalogue
unfinished knitting
sachets of perfume
      hipflask of whiskey

a packed church: the chosen
hymns, the usual psalm, glowing
eulogy, slow drive
      to the pre-paid plot

the wake, held at her Club:
open bar, finger food,
a happy-snap slide show
      spinning tales . . .

He is loosely held together
by the woollen cardigan
she knitted for him
      before the rift;

She settles in beside him in her best
blue dress, clipped at the throat
with a marcasite brooch
      his 'I'm sorry' gift.

Inside the dark casket
her mouth, stitched into a smile
for the viewing,
      comes undone . . .

Missing

Heather Warne

I wasn't expecting them to bring you back to us in a bag—a small body bag that hid the truth of what had just occurred. Not only that, there were two bags: the inner one white and plastic—in case of leakage, they said. I thought you would be laying completely still but visible in the cat bed you liked to nap in—the one we especially took with us to bring you home in.

I sat in the car with the weight of you, still warm, on my lap. But I couldn't see you. Instead I stared at gold paw prints stamped onto black biodegradable material with matching gold ribbon tying the bag shut in three places. And I felt thwarted when my instinct was to drink you in, to stroke your fur and talk to you, to say goodbye again, to be with what was left of you.

We carried you back to the heart of our home where an hour before you had gobbled from my hand a few choice morsels of barbecued chicken, your all time favourite, and where you relaxed, just a bit, as I brushed you ever so carefully and we took a few last photos, your eyes milky and unseeing.

Straight away I grabbed the kitchen scissors and sliced open the bags so we could at last look at you. The other animals, the ones you latterly distained, came sniffing. I read somewhere that it's good to let them do that; it will help them understand your absence.

I understood, too, now that I could see you utterly and irreversibly still. We didn't look at all of you, somehow it was too late for that; something had been stolen by the bags. We hurried so as not to have to bury you in the dark.

That final moment, when the green liquid raced down the plastic tube, was so quick like turning off a light switch. I felt your tortured muscles let go under my hands and you were gone.

Your absence is big. I cannot bear to think about you cold and wet in the bottom of that hole under the loquat tree, the weight of sodden earth pressing down. I haven't looked until today; it's been dark by the time I get home. The flowers I bought along with the chicken are still fresh, preserved by the cold. It was raining when I stood there this morning, drips ricocheting loudly from the leaves around you.

The clickety clack of your paws on the floor is missing, your drinking bowl sits quietly, no more lap lap, clinkety clink, as the tags on your collar hit the side.

It's been a while since we went for a walk or you sought out my lap, too sore or nervy to sit there, but your fur will stay forever silky in my hands and my heart will go on holding you.

The Grey Goose
Nikki McWatters

The bird arrived with the winter frosts. We heard him first—deep, harrowing hacks as if he was an old man suffering from a cold. The goose gargled out a noise that was part cough, part cry. He shuffled along the sidewalk outside the shops, barking out the sounds that stretched over an octave, a sad cacophony of grief. His mate was dead. Janet from the pharmacy came down and told us the female had been hit by a car.

'He's singing their song,' she explained.

The ruffled, grey goose was mourning his girl.

'These birds mate for life,' Janet said, folding her arms, shaking her head. 'And they have this duet, their own special song, his part and hers and if one dies, the other sings the whole song to keep it alive.'

We watched him folding his head down beneath a loop of neck to peck at his wing. He waddled north up Main Street and then south doing a sentry run along the shops and always with the honking opera of loss. His dark eyes seemed to seek out the spirit of his lost mate. As the cars whizzed by, he startled nervously and wound up his song even louder until I felt it rattle into my bones. It was the saddest sound. Primal. Disturbing.

I tried to feed him some stale bread from the back room but he stared at my outstretched hand, momentarily quiet, and then he padded his webbed feet away from me for another march along the footpath, singing.

'Arrrrunk. Arrrunk,' he cried, his long black feathered neck straining as if he was listening to some invisible orchestra. His eyes were mud-brown and glistened and I wondered if geese cried tears.

'It will be alright,' I said, as he passed.

I took some currants from my pocket on the second day and sat patiently with my hand outstretched while he honked by, lost in his own world of emptiness, a vacuum that he filled with sound. At first I found it grating, annoying and uncomfortable. Geese are no larks and sad sounds make bitter music. The other store owners threatened to chase him away with a broom, banishing him to the pond down in Rotary Park.

By Day Three the song had become familiar to me. Its cadence and rhythm had margins and structure. The notes were carefully selected and rose with a clear crescendo. I began to mark where the song finished and began again.

On Day Five I tried to sing along. The goose stopped and cast a curious gaze over me. His eyes seemed to understand that his pain mattered to me. He took some currants from my hand, his beak tickling over my skin. He let me touch his soft feathered head.

The next day, there was silence. The old grey goose flew away, his wings wide and his flight-path steady. He had gone in search of a new song.

Just Me
Jo Parker

It has been sixteen years since you died and here I am, still trying to get over it. When you died my grief cast an emotional web over my life which has caught every letting go in its grip since then.

And there has been so much letting go. As time has marched forward from your death I have struggled to keep up. Our boys, the most beautiful and painful part of my life since you died, have marched too quickly for me. Every day a steady progression toward what has now come. Without you, and in spite of me, our boys have grown up.

Without you here to help me I have succeeded and failed in guiding them through every precious moment of their childhoods. Now their childhoods are over and I'm forced to let go again. But I'm not ready. They are my connection to you, to the me who was with you. I thought I would always be mothering our two boys. And, yes, I am still their mum, but I'll never lie with one of them on each arm as the sweet smell of my babies fills my nostrils. That won't happen ever again.

Instead I lie in bed and try unsuccessfully to cry myself dry. Silent sobs so no one can hear what a small distance I have really come since you died. So long ago that I can't even use it as an excuse for my sadness anymore. This pain has become so much a part of me now that I can't even separate it out and call it grief. Grief is a response to something that happens but this pain just feels like it is me.

I had no idea when you died how it would change who I was. I have become two women. One is so hurt and damaged from watching you die and nursing two babies through the long nights of loneliness that she can barely get up in the morning. The other is a mum of three, with a new partner, a job, a smile, who goes out to dinner with friends and says 'I'm good' when people ask how she is.

Unfortunately, though, I am not really the woman who smiles. I am the woman crying alone in bed who hasn't let go. I am the one who blames herself for the scars that your death and my grief have left on our boys' lives. Who can't accept that I lost years of their beautiful, brief childhoods to the grief of losing you. Who feels that I could have been a better mum, a better person, if I could just have let you go.

But I don't even know what I am letting go of anymore. I thought my grief was about letting go of you, that grief is a response to something that happens. Now this pain feels like it is me, like I will always be waiting for another thing to get caught in the web.

Glass
Mary Jones

I remember your voice, the sound of your laughter,
our voices in the scullery, bubbling over the sink.
You washed, I dried, we argued, both of us claiming
the right to be Sheriff of Nottingham. The suds
overflowed as we swashed and buckled. Mum
heaved sighs, brought the mop for the floor.
Most of the time you gave in, settled for Errol Flynn,
let me be Basil Rathbone.

I remember the smell of polish worked into floor tiles
ready for us to go skating with dusters tied on our feet,
the lazy silence along the canal as you sat
and fished, the feel of the bread that I squished
and rolled on my hands into pellets for ground-bait,
carefully lobbed where you pointed, Mum banished
to search for bullrushes, because you said
her talking frightened the fish.

I don't remember your funeral—I wasn't there.
Mum said I was too young, it wasn't
considered appropriate. I was sent off to school
on the train that rainy morning. I remember
the kindly touch of a hand on my shoulder,
the teacher who told me I needn't go with the others
into Assembly. I stood by the window, feeling
the glass cold under my palm, seeing
nothing.

For Stephanie, Johannesburg 1974
Marion Dundon

I still see your face, small with bright dark eyes watching me. In a bed in a room with white walls. Then you turned towards the light from the window on our right. You lie in my arms soft and warm. Your skin still perfect, but for a deep red birthmark on your eyelid. I remember those black luminous eyes. My little owl.

The night they said you had died, in a room away from me, two short nurses walked in with a small silver tray.

'A needle to make you feel better.'

'No.'

A few days later.

I stand at the window of our bedroom on the day of your burial watching the rain. The wind tosses the tree outside and the weaver bird's nest, dangling from a branch, sways. Only a week before, the little yellow bird had finished it.

We had watched as she carried long leaves and tore them into strips to weave a nest with a roof and a little opening at the base.

The summer rain splashes into the room. Before I close the window, I stretch my arms out the window into the rain.

I look to the sky and tell you, 'you didn't live for nothing. It wasn't nothing. You were here.'

I am wearing a long, black dress with little white flowers and my breasts are bound tight with white cotton from a torn up sheet, safety pins under the bodice, to try and stop the milk.

Then it's time to go.

After the funeral, friends say you must go away together and have a holiday.

'That will be good for you and we'll babysit your little girl.'

I stand in an airport washroom in Capetown. The taps on, water running over my hands, then the tears start down my face. A woman walks in and turns to me,

'Are you okay?'

'My baby died,' I say.

Quickly she turns and walks through the door.

The shame, how could I do that to a stranger? My grief is making me a fool.

A few months later, I'm in Zambia in a living room in Ndola, a copper mining town.

Women and children, young expat European wives of geologists and engineers working on water supplies for villages and copper mines. Everywhere I go there are babies. Two new babies in the room. My three year old daughter watches them, then, holding my knees she looks up and gives me the words,

'Our baby died didn't she, mummy?'

'Yes,' I say.

Lourdes
David Grant Lloyd

Catholic Healthcare
        agapanthus uncut
        and bottle brush
The Blessed Mary figure
        adjacent to the stairway

He ripped out the cannula
from both his forearms
bleeding out excessively
soaking the bed sheets
His grip was still strong

Western Plains Security
        on tinted windows
Staff smiling politely
        passing through
        the corridors
A vending machine: Out of Order

He tried for the catheter
The nurses screamed, *No!*
        all the time
listening to ABC Jazz
His face: Greek tragedy
Allergy: Endone

The main entry
        visitor parking
        fire hydrants
and bike racks
Over the stone wall
        A plaque reads:
        Lloyd Beetson Memorial
Ibises walk over the rose garden

Black on White
Bill Bean

He sat on the red plastic chair in the polished vinyl whiteness. The doctor, muppet-like in green clothes and softly scuffling bootees came to the waiting room and his set face said the words before he spoke. She had died. The operation had been too much. Black words in white light.

The reasons came with professional concern but it didn't matter. She had gone. They had come in together with optimism in her suitcase and now she was ever to stay. All the important words would now be unspoken and he was adrift in a place he could not comprehend. There had been an understanding that this could be an outcome but they had not admitted it. The paperwork cemented it all to reality. Sign here . . . and here. Black writing on white. And community support is two doors down the corridor.

He left. Fumbling the keys in the car door and sitting on the asphalt of the carpark as the emptiness grew bigger, then driving out of town to the house, closed and cold, two cups left in the drying rack, a coat not taken over a chair back, shadows of her presence.

The mechanics of living were demanding and what she had done in the partnership was unusual for him and when he did her tasks his grief was almost unbearable. He packed her clothes and cried as he smelt and felt the softness that was left behind. The tangibles had gone and he sought some comfort in the photographs but there was no sound or feel or smell, just black on white. He cried for a long time, his pain a burning scald and it was only exhaustion that softened the edges of the hurt. And then it was all gone and he found some solace in the remembering.

The kids came and were uneasy at his grief. He was a father figure brought low, abdicating his authority, not willing any more to argue or resist their instructions and recommendations and they felt unsure. They urged him sell the farm, pack up, move away, start something new, forget. They couldn't understand the depth, they had lost a reference point, he had lost a lifetime. And so he stayed, for his anchor to the years and her memory could be refreshed by the silent contemplation of place.

He kept up the small rituals they had had and looked behind as he went his way. In the garden he was expectant for a presence but it was all gone. The habits weren't just props to hold his life together, they were part of his being.

He would take his morning coffee on the verandah and the view to the river and across the paddocks to the ranges was the same as when she was there and he understood that although they had been together, they were separate. Travellers on a journey. And he had to finish the trip alone.

Consummation

I wanted you buried deep
safe
warm

you hated to be cold

they planned to leave you suspended

other mourners had to leave
before they would lower you
and I could see you home

I had learned from the first time
when we walked away from our son

hanging suspended
with fake grass and plastic flowers
hiding the earth mound
that would be his coverlet

I never saw him to his grave
that little white box
floated in my dreams

Vivian Garner

The Body Mother Made Me
Maria Vouis

The body mother made me
        remembers her.
My lips, her smile stretched across sorrow
and one tooth lost with each child born.

The body she seeded for me
        knows her.
Nine Greek moons to grow, twelve more to suck,
years to wean and teethe and cry.

These breasts she planted as buds
        bloom for her,
flower in my veiled night movements,
swell at full moon with her secret musk.

These feet she fashioned for me
        danced for her,
in her mountain village square,
stepped the map of her maiden soles.

The hands mother kneaded me
        labour for her.
My hands pull wild greens, stir her pot,
my fingers light the lamp of the dead.

This voice she gifted me
        keens for her,
Doric modes hummed into my breath,
ocean hymns of leaving but always coming home.

These eyes mother lent light to
        look for her.
My eyes leak her tears now,
now that she is dissolved to bone.

All We Have Lost
Peter J. Wells

When we crossed through the barbed wire we left behind nothing; our buildings were rubble, our jobs gone, our hospitals bombed. All our friends were gone. My mother-in-law had died, she was the last of our parents; but we still had each other, one loss we were too tired to face, so we left.

I was one of many, though many people know my face. We did not expect the man to be waiting with his camera. We were scared his presence would alert the guards but he put his finger to his lips, pointed to the nearly full moon and whispered in Arabic, 'no flash, the moon is enough.' I held apart two strands and my wife climbed through. Her dress caught on one of the barbs, a small tear, but she was unharmed. Then I passed our baby into her open hands.

I heard him taking pictures. The camera was quiet but every movement seemed loud enough to bring the guards. My wife held the wire so I could climb through. The man said, 'I shall take you to the camp.' On the way he showed me a picture on the small screen at the back of his camera, of me handing our baby through the wire. My wife's face was hidden but my face seemed to show every emotion: anger, confusion and disappointment, even joy. I saw these things and they seemed to merge into one another, and then to disappear.

The next day the man came to the camp. He was looking for me. He said, 'your picture has been printed in newspapers all over the world.' I did not think much of it. My world was our tent, the same as all the others, and our ration of food and water.

One year later the man came to the camp again. He spoke in Arabic but I replied in English. Opportunities for conversation were difficult to find. There was some hope we would find refuge in Australia, and I wanted to practice.

In the camp hope can be dangerous, such places bring out our worst, our old rivalries and jealousies, only my wife knew I was learning English. So I kept my voice quiet and hoped he would follow suit. He handed me a cut out square of newspaper. There was my picture and another picture of him in a black and white suit holding a trophy. He said that the picture he took had won a prize. I could tell he was proud and we shared a cup of tea.

When he left there was room to think about this. It sounds silly but I wondered if the meaning of my life was reduced to this picture. When I was gone, perhaps my child would see the picture and remember her father; then I asked myself, 'what will she know of all we have lost?'

It was then I decided to write down our story, if only to bear witness.

Design
Catherine Wright

my summer's come to mud
I need different shoes
I need trouser protectors
it clarts my clothes and every
step is chosen with worms in mind

the trees are full of treachery
one moment russet-robed next
discarding leaves, disgusted
convinced by wind that
somehow it is better to
be bare, leaving birds
beached on desert bones
in the chill

I wish I could toss leaves
a tree salad against the grey but
these have turned to sog
one moment's glisten on
the ground, then
glove-glue stuck

and it's not just me
above, geese stream in
shifting calligraphy, their
punctured cries design my
dreams, remind me
my friend is dying

Veteran
Anthony Lawrence

When things were bad, my uncle's own backyard seemed
the corner of a prisoner
        of war camp in the Philippines.
              Even the nectar birds he whistled up
into a captive audience could warble
like a man sleep-deprived and delusional
        in the rags of his confinement.
              The bird bath gave back its oval of sky
the way polished tin, hammered to a tent pole
        could return the face of a soldier,
            when shaving.
The history of anxiety among veterans of war
includes a list of euphemisms, conditions with names
        that define and sanitize trauma:
            Nostalgia, Soldier's Heart, Railway Spine
and *Shell Shock*. He came home with *Battle Fatigue*,
which caused him to stutter mid-sentence
        and grimace over some throwaway comment
            as though he were taking offence.
He wasn't. War had stripped the filter
from the language of his body, and his nerves
        went haywire. He didn't live to see
            yet another name for his affliction: *PTSD*
in television documentaries, anywhere
men and women returned to break like news.
        In his last years he turned privacy
            to reclusiveness, and then became
invisible as the bul-buls that had once called
his garden home. On Anzac Day his medals
        remained on felt in the box
            he kept in a cupboard.
He'd listen to the parade on a radio, a roll-call
of mates under the flag of his Division.
        From Sydney to Sandakan
            and back, grief beyond definition.

The Breaker Bar
Christina M. Aitken

A teenaged girl in white
sings sunset hues
with a voice like
sand and wind

In front of me
another girl writhes to the rhythms
from her wheelchair
clapping and sucking her fingers
I watch her put a serviette in her mouth
At first, I don't think past the wine in my hand
but wonder if — she might choke
I tell her mother
They're sisters, she says
leaning in too close with
relief and wine-kissed breath

Meningitis

Her smile stretches thin
from the barstool
to the wheelchair

The girl comes to the end of her set
and asks for requests.

I ask her if she knows 'Cry me a river'.

A Confession
G. Vickers

'What are we going to do about that cough?' the nurse asked, as though to a sick child, fussing with the pillows behind you. It had been getting worse and you were bent double to weather this latest paroxysm.

'I don't know,' you responded, seriously. You looked pale and confused. I could tell you wanted to give a better answer, to turn it over in your mind until you saw a solution, as you would have done in better days. But the fentanyl clouded your thoughts and you were deeply battle weary.

I sat in a shabby hospital chair and paid silent audience to this, just another drab accessory in the pastel-and-beige room where you would soon die. I was unable to help.

This is not my only unforgivable act.

I was by the ocean when you were brought truly low. With childish abandon we had fled suburbia and the hospitals and the sickness. We had sat on the shore by night looking out across the horizon and we were electrified by the vast, roaring spectacle in purple and grey. We relished this unearned distance from the cancer.

Driving back, my calls went unanswered. When finally I got through, I learned that while I was gone, you had suffered: you had tried to walk, had lost control, had fallen and hit your head. You had always used your words and your strength to protect and work for me, and, then, when I was most able, I had given you nothing of the same in return.

One of the last times you ever left your bed, I squatted by your chair and rested my head against your broad forearm. Like an old lion, dignified and inscrutable, you sat and took in the final view you would have of the outside world: it was mostly a concrete parking lot. This was not a prospect fit for a king. Your only concern was that my temperature seemed high.

I didn't stay with you through those last nights. I will therefore never know if you were thirsty or cold or bothered by your vivid dreams and the myoclonic jerks that woke you from them. I will never know if you lay there feeling the suffocating inevitability of the palliative care ward. I was weak in ways you would never have been, with the roles reversed.

You never once complained. You said that I was smart and beautiful whenever you could.

I want to go home. But because you're gone, I never can again. I'm assaulted by an urge that grinds, bones-deep: to be with you again just as we were that night, up country. Sitting together on the veranda, the darkness alive around us and the new year upon us, I felt so young and you felt so permanent. Neither of us knew what was coming yet. You were talking about your life and I wasn't listening closely enough.

We none of us deserved you.

I didn't understand this before.

The Glove

Viktoria Rendes

I find a brown leather glove in your bedside drawer. It is bent into the shape of your hand. If I am careful, I can slip my hand around it, just as if I were holding yours.

I remember the bitter cold Swiss winter, walking along icy tracks, ankle deep in snow and reaching out for your gloved hand as I slipped. I clutched for it as my feet gave way and laughed as you pulled me up so I could right myself. I held on for dear life, for comfort and support and toddled along next to you, hand in glove.

My own gloves never take on the shape of my hand the way yours did. Mine sit flat, are scrunched in a pocket or are folded neatly, one into the other, for safekeeping. They may be warm but they offer no comfort.

For a long time, I would return to feel the contour of that glove. Every now and then, I felt a need for its weight in my hand when everything around me seemed weightless and ready to float away. The shape was solid, something I could hold onto.

At times, your glove felt like a sculpture of a hand begging, reaching out for me to place something in your palm. Much later, it reminded me of a death mask, an imprint made by memory with no muscle within to make it move. It was your hand that made it take on its shape in life, and now it has retained its shape in death.

I no longer know where that glove is. All I know is that I would never have discarded it. I have opened boxes in quiet panic, looked in suitcases, drawers, bags but still haven't been able to locate it. All that remains is the memory of the glove and the memory of the person who once wore it.

It is all that ever remains.

Whatever Darkness Brings
Kristen Roberts

Last night's sky has been unwrapped,
the stars have been discarded.
Dawn will show gums bare-limbed and blushing,
the roads will hiss beneath passing cars
and we'll be left to unravel
the ink-spill of sadness that ribbons inside us.

I curl against your back,
two question marks aligned
as we fall into the fracturing night.
When the lightning licks only
the lowest curves of the sky,
we lose our contours to the gloom
but I take whatever the darkness brings
as long as it still holds you.

The Ticket
Vanessa Ives

When authorities found the remains of Stephen's missing brother after years of searching, it was clear that he had committed suicide.

Our marriage was strong, but as the months crawled by, I watched Stephen's behaviour change. His anxiety, dizzying emotional highs and deep lows led to a diagnosis of bipolar depression. He lost his job.

The doctors worked hard to prove their care. Electroconvulsive therapy delivered a pocket full of smiles, but tore gaps in memories of happier days.

My faith dissolved over time, as medicos' discursive snatches and grabs at scientific explanations blended into frontier sophistry.

Our local mental health unit placed a daily watch on Stephen; small comfort when I had to go on a business trip. In the space of a day, while I was on the other side of the country, a bean counter scaled back visits to every second day. They didn't inform me.

Stephen saw his opportunity.

I arrived home late after a long flight. The lights were ablaze. Paramedics trundled their gear to and fro in a glaze of reflective clothing. I staggered to the door. The ambulance crew stopped me. I pushed past them until a young paramedic girl took my hand and led me upstairs to the bedroom.

Stephen lay curled on the floor, his blue-grey eyes open. His pupils seemed to widen; the only movement I could perceive. I touched his eyelids and stared into those widening orbs.

'Pupillary sphincter dilation,' said an older paramedic standing behind me.

'Get out!' I yelled.

I collapsed upon my deceased husband, pressing my body against his; it felt like the shortest half hour that will last a lifetime.

Curse those pushing tears. I knew they could burst any moment into a torrent of sadness for how his meagre 42 years was treated, how his talents were discarded, how his cries for help were ignored by his abusive parents.

I gazed into his eyes; pupils as planets, spheres of intellect, worlds of wonder and uniqueness now fading to nothing and so curiously alluring.

Someone laughed downstairs. I heard shuffling and muffled conversations that trailed outside.

I got up awkwardly and stood at the top of the stairs. I wanted to throw myself down with a force that would smash the tall window at the foot of the stairs. Caught between desperately wanting to be with him and ashamed of self-preservation, I slowly retracted my foot from the ledge.

I turned towards Stephen's slumped body and spotted what looked like a crumpled train ticket under the bed.

I reached for it, flicking a couple of Jim Beam bottles aside. A teardrop tapped the card; a product description for his medication. In the hazy jumble of words, one sentence screamed at me: 'Caution: overdose will result in coma'.

The information was clear.

His doctor knew it too.

His doctor had handed my husband a ticket. The local mental health unit provided the pass.

Stephen took his trip into peace the only way he could.

Meeting Valerie
Adrienne Hunter

She meets us at the arrivals gate at the airport in Vienna. We recognise her straight away even though we haven't seen her before. She holds up an Australian flag and holds back tears. I hug my brother's ex-girlfriend. Mum hugs her son's ex-girlfriend and Valerie hugs us back—the sister and mother of her dead ex-boyfriend.

She drives us to our hotel and then we walk together to a restaurant. With appealing warmth and Austrian directness she tells us about reading the email Mum sent her. She asks questions. What happened? How did he do it? Why had we taken nearly six months to let her know?

Valerie meets us the next morning and takes us on a walking tour of her city. We admire the elegant buildings, the cafes, the history but stumble over our emotions. She spent a lot of time in Australia and she loves our wild land and strange creatures. So different to the ordered, cultured Austrian capital.

At night we go ice-skating in front of the town hall. For a couple of hours we forget and float—weaving around the large rink that is lit up with fairy lights. I know why he loved her. She is warm, sociable, fun, curious and resilient. I wish she didn't have to know this pain, horror, guilt, regret and sorrow.

I learn more about my brother. She tells us he was thoughtful, thoughtless, romantic, loving and distant. She loved him. He broke her heart many times. And now he's done it again, one final time. We are connected by love and tragedy and separated by vast distance and despair. How do I say good-bye to a never-to-be-sister-in-law? We walk with heavy bags and hurting hearts to the departure gate.

Auf Wiedersehen, Valerie. *Auf Wiedersehen* and *vielen Dank*.

Babe
Rob Wallis

in memory of Ron Cadd

The invisible blade of cancer has scored
pain into his face, cuts into bone.
Skin is stretched over the skull's drum.
He lists to the left. Morphine patches
allow snapshots of his former self
to reappear. *How are ya babe?*
I try to resist an indulgent answer.
This is not about me. I am here
to savour the conundrum of a man's life.
Conversation slips into the blindfolded
firing-line of doctors, appointments,
results of tests, crumbling milestones
at shorter, and shorter distances.
A change to the subject of my social week
is laced with irrelevance, and guilt.
But he wants to know. Wants
to touch life reeling through its paces
beyond the walls of his hospitalised home.
Yet anything I say triggers the switch
back to the visits of the palliative nurse,
the family, wanted or unwanted friends.
As I leave he holds me in a smile.
It's been good to see ya babe. Our hug
entangles us in the complexity of hope.
And he's holding on, as if letting go
would sever a link with the animate world.

Chops

Alexandra Gordon

Chops: I met him when I started school,
I was five
He had that smile that dogs get   that unconditional love

He never gave up hoping   the mangy mutt
that someone would love him back

1 eye   1 ear   3 legs
    damaged goods
a reminder of the ability to break

Who would

He had a certain charm
a friendliness that hadn't been cut out
    his trust despite his abuse   his unrequited loyalty   his willingness

He lived with the Rosiers   Emma loved him   while he was a puppy
'till he lost his eye to the burglar   then he was brave   but ugly

Then he got run over   lost his leg
Was made even uglier by his limp
    loved a little less

Still he hoped

Then he lived with the Jacobs family
    lost his ear in a fight with their dog Scruffy
now hideous   I was ten

They left him at a shelter the next year

We found him there after Spot died—we were looking for a replacement
    Chops limped over licked my hand
        remembered me

we didn't take him though

I think about Chops sometimes   his matted black and white fur
    crumpled lid covering the empty eye-socket
missing bits   scars   hopeful smile

He saw it all through his one good eye

Watched us drive away   He ran behind the car for a moment with
lopsided abandon
   wagged his tail   hopefully   and smiled with the fathomless
   forgiveness of a dog.

Focus on the Car
Catherine Moffat

Focus on the car. A white Toyota Corolla strung somewhere between heaven and hell. A car in a tree. 50 metres down a cliff with 350 more to fall.

Focus on the helicopter, on the swish, whir whir of the blades. Focus on the rescue team abseiling down towards you. Focus on the watchers on the cliff.

Focus on the ropes. The ties that bind. The knots that slip. The slipknot. The noose. The Gordian knot. The reef, the hitch, the half bend. Granny's knot. Ropes to tie you down. Ropes to pull you back.

Focus on the night. The cicada sounds. The distant wash of highway noise rising and flowing like an ocean.

Focus on the headlights. Still shining out impossibly, illuminating a green arc of leaves, the next day, when they found you.

Focus on the broken fences. On the sense of purpose that sent you through not one but two safety barriers.

Focus on the policeman who came to my door. 'Are you the owner of . . . ?' 'Did he have your permission to use your car?' Focus on his shoes. Those black, highly polished boots. That neat double stitching.

Focus on the car. Do we push it down or haul it up? Do we leave it hanging, rusting out piece by piece, on and on until an inevitable end? Do we let it loose to fly for a moment before it smashes on the forest floor below?

Focus on the car.

Focus anywhere but on your sweet, beautiful, damaged face, your beautiful damaged life.

Make-up Lessons
Maya Linden

My sister, who taught me how to gently shade the corners of my eyes so no one could tell I'd cried all night. A careful dab of bronzer with her finger on my lids kept secret to the world that my heart was breaking.

I remembered this again in the weeks after she died but I could never get it right. The morning she died, I couldn't believe that I'd ever cried for something so unworthy as being dumped by a guy. I'd thought my heart was broken then but that was just a dent.

My sister, who saw the world in exactly the same way I did. One late night, driving home from a party, we were stopped at a red light for what felt like hours. We looked around us, the roads were dark and deserted. The light stayed firmly red.

We jokingly decided that we must have died in an accident at the intersection and would be there together, caught forever in the moment before our death. Just as we settled in for eternity the light turned green again.

My sister, who really is dead now. And I don't know where to find her. Although I feel her presence close by sometimes, when I drive, and Tiny Dancer comes on the radio and a static spark bounces off my fingers the way it did from her skin while I held her hand in the hospital as her energy slipped.

And I smile and say hello and tell her things that would make her laugh: updates on fashion, celebrities and TV shows, how Bruce Jenner really did become a woman, that Donald Trump is president. And all the things she's missed: that I got married on the beach, like we'd always talked of, and had a baby girl as I'd always dreamed.

My sister, who never missed my birthday, who still made her way, so thin and feverish, to my restaurant dinner four months before she died.

Now three birthdays have come and gone without her; with no event to mark them but her silence and I'm the age that she will always be.

Oh, my sister, who never wanted us to worry. Who never talked about her suffering, lest it make us suffer. If only I could be as strong as you were in the face of death. As resilient to despair.

Perhaps one day I will think only of the way things were—days by the pool and seaside, your smile and tanned skin, your thick, shiny hair; our private jokes and the secrets we promised to keep until the end—but applying eye shadow to tear stained lids is all I can hope to master until then.

The Day Before
Janet C. Fraser

Inhabit the space
When I can barely inhabit myself
Heart thudding tugging to be
Free of this body.
Last coffee drunk before tomorrow's coffee
Breath slow to make each breath not the last one
Before tomorrow
Blue sky beautiful
Dead baby still not here.
Still not three nor playing with her siblings
They ask often what she would be doing
She is always reckoned in the family sums
She is always the jagged hole in the black ice
Of my heart
The tears on my face right now even in public
Grief doesn't tidy away like socks
Or even hide in the third drawer down
In the kitchen where the other mystery items lie
Discomfit clear on the faces around me
Distancing to avoid the fumes of my sour grief
Peer at me through laced fingers
No bargaining keeps relentless death at bay
Best to stop turn face embrace
This will be my lifelong relationship
Who is brave enough to witness our nuptials

My Father Comes to the Island
Renee Pettitt-Schipp

we turn it between us
the new shape
of him

in gentle morning light
I see him dressing, through his
half-opened door
reading in stark ribs
what neither one of us
can say

my father
once amphibian, his swimmer's feet
now numb, crash into coral
leaving him to limp
and bleed for days

my father comes to the island
pulls cap over new sight of scalp
though we both know
what's written
under there

standing by the wire
he and I watch his plane come in
I hold him closer than ever
he walks away from me
and still I don't say
I don't say
a thing.

Lay Grievers
Linda Harding

'Is she gone?' my mother asks me, as another rattling breath escapes the gaping mouth of my grandmother. Nana's head is cradled in her arms, once more the infant. 'Is she gone?'

My mother thinks I might know if that breath was the last. All of us who are gathered round this dying 89-year-old matriarch, whom we loved, want it to be over, need it to be done, and all eyes are on my answer, which is, 'I don't know'.

How could I know? This is no sterile ward. It is just us. We are at home. That final breath comes when it comes, not one tormenting second sooner.

I watch my mother regress, become a child again. She is pared back with grief. She calls my Nana 'Mummy'. 'Oh Mummy!' She is a distraught 5 year old who needs comforting. I am the parent she looks to for guidance in this terrible moment: the final orphaning. Death shuffles roles. I am inadequate.

We are all inadequate, the six siblings, and their families, gathered round this bed. We are all in new territory. It does not matter if we have seen death before or kept vigil at a million bedside farewells; we are novices with the departure of this unique human being who loomed so large in our hearts. We feel inadequate to navigate our own grief, let alone each other's. It is just the way it is.

That was indeed the last breath. The tears come pouring out. We lean on each other and sob, tissues passed around, noses blown. Someone leaves the bedroom to make a phone call to relatives not here. There's an irresistible impulse to tell someone else, as if making the call will be making this real.

Shell-shocked, we leave the shell of my grandmother alone in her bed. We go to the living room, which is where we want to live. Not here among the dead. We make tea. We talk about her.

While sipping, sniffing, laughing at some memory, we realize the funeral home staff will come to get her body soon. She is still wearing her jewelry. No one wants to go back to that room, but my cousin and I volunteer.

We walk in to find rigor has set in to the empty body of my grandmother; we have to struggle with her fingers to remove the rings. We speak to her tenderly, apologize profusely for our fumbling and neglect. We have not laid her out.

In hospitals they know these things: lay the body straight, remove clothes and cleanse it, dress it for burial. But, here, saying goodbye at home, desperate to be free of pain and death's proximity, we have forgotten this last service to the loved dead.

I lean into her soft white hair and whisper one last apology. I kiss her cold forehead. It is a sacred moment.

I know she forgives us all: the lay grievers, who did not lay her out.

Blue

Verity Laughton

1.

Look how the silk shroud of the sea
is edge to edge with that far shout of
sky. The sky's a thing flung so
clean and high that the idle birds,
surfing for echo, wheel and cry,
pulsing its impossible   blue,

only to float   down

to the sheeny sea, softer than down,
notes, that's all, each a moment,

                          sounded.

Or is it a loom? On the benign
horizon, is that a line of blue, barred
by bolts of steamy, shuffled sun,
where seabirds shuttle up to light
and down again to blue?

No. This sky's nor song nor
craft for cloth for covering.

No. It's a body of blue – long ribs
of blue, straight thighs of blue,
cool curve of bony back of
blue. Oh you. The bird knocks
in your breast. Rest.

2.

Step through the hinged dark. Cold calls you down.

Shadow blossoms like bruised rose, like a de-shelled star, like

smoke in a jar. There is no bell of being human

here, just a cage of silence that waits with the

door   unlocked.

3.

I seem to see you always just ahead of me, your moth-soft dress, your limbs like cobweb, the rasp of your breath in this strange air that sits in the lungs like hot loose
                                                                                                 ash.

I lose you, then there is a flicker in the silent trees ahead and –

I stretch   because   it seems   that   it would take   just that   one   stretch   but   it

never does

                    and   you never do   look back.

Fragments

Annie Barrett

2014 Remembering my father

My father died this day, 40 years ago. Grand Final Day. He slipped away; high blood pressure, a burst aneurysm. Like a valve going off, it erupted. What had kept the lid on? His body took over. Enough. Tired of living, 53. We gathered around his hospital bed. At home that night I looked at the moon. I was 17; 17 years with him, 40 years without.

2014 My friend

My friend is dying; 40 years of adult friendship, our first 17 childhood years unknown. I wake up sad. Morning tears come. They keep coming. Not like a burst aneurysm, blood spilling into the brain, leaking into any possible spaces. My tears leak, but they have space. They come. They slide down the aging skin on my face and dry. I give them space. I don't mind grief, but now it is raw again and it shakes me. Fear.

My mother

My mother died three years after my father. Did she follow him? Ovarian cancer cells, the silent stalkers, crept around her body. Multiplying, living. Then came first-generation chemotherapy. 'Too much,' she whispered. 'They have given me too much.' Nearly her last words. What were they doing giving her chemo as she lay dying? 'It is not visiting hours,' a fierce matron scolded me. She did not want to let me in. Again, we gathered around another hospital bed. A last visit, more whispered words she could not speak. Her light extinguished.

2014 My sister

She sleeps finally, after her footsteps pad down the hallway again and again. Hopefully fluids and toxins are shed along with those pesky cancer cells, gobbled up by more chemotherapy and spat out, down the toilet. The nurses wear blue gowns, purple gloves and protective glasses on the day ward. So many people; some well, some frail, some with short regrowth of hair, some take photos of their last chemo. Finished. But how do they know it is all over, health the winner? Loss of appetite, stinging fingers, weight loss, no energy. She gets off lightly. She manages the ravages of side effects well, but to no avail.

2015 My friend

I lie listening, waiting. Another breath comes after so long. Rising. Falling. A spider scurries along near the ceiling, now along the carpet. All is quiet outside. All around me is her dreaming; the blue bedroom walls are filled with her fabric art. Irish Madonna Celtic dreaming, hand-dyed silk gum leaves and a brilliant red and deep olive landscape. A truck rumbles by and her dying bed pulses it's ripples, holding her frailty. Rising. Falling. Will today be her last? Will her spirit fly free?

2016 My Sister

All treatments have failed now and still her fingers sting. Is death calling this time? In my mind I prepare for her death. My heart hurts, afraid to hope. Miraculously, a new drug pumps through her veins. She lives. My heavy heart wants to trust, wants to soar once more.

Numbing the Heart
Miya Dawn

I was sitting in my boyfriend's bedroom smoking cigarettes and listening to old rock albums in the usual way we spent our days.

His house was depressive. It was always dirty, bed linen was never changed, bathrooms were filthy and there was always a pile of used dishes in the sink. His mother was an alcoholic teacher who had been married to a man who bred dogs. Because of her condition she wouldn't care for her house or children the way I was used to. Maybe she became like that after the divorce, I don't know.

The worst part of his house was the backyard that they transformed into a kennel. They had three or four dogs there (not sure anymore as many of my memories faded since) living in terrible conditions. The kennel was like a jail and it hadn't been cleaned for several years, probably since the divorce, so the stink and the flies lived there with them.

My boyfriend's bedroom window faced the kennel, the shit and the smell so it was always closed except sometimes to let the smoke of our many cigarettes out. There was nothing to look at from that window.

I was fifteen, two days to be sixteen and I had been with him for about seven months now. Why would I choose such a disruptive home I don't know, maybe it was due to the last year's decline of my own reality. Being there and with him was like an angry, silent scream.

His mum opened the door and came in.

'Your mother called and you need to go home, they need to talk to you . . . You'll have to be strong . . . .'

Her kind tone alerted me as she had never liked me much. I knew that tone. Something powerful had happened.

I didn't need to go home to know what it was. I knew what I was going to be told. He had finally done it. This was the moment I had already imagined several times, that kept me awake for so many nights since I was maybe thirteen, that made me pray when I didn't believe in God.

I went home anyway because I had to. Things have to follow their course.

My boyfriend took me on his motorbike. Along the way my system immediately started building self defence walls and I was already rehearsing how was I going to react to the news that wasn't news because I already knew what happened, and how do you react spontaneously to something shocking that is not a surprise anymore?

Thinking how I was going to react, instead of thinking about the fact itself, did not allow me to feel the reality of my father's suicide.

It was in that moment, those thirty minutes since I was told I had to go home to receive some news until I arrived home, that another me was born. I had split in two. One to keep living and one to take the pain.

Why
Leith Reid

there are all the children that toddle and tucked
babies in wraps and prams and five year olds asking
why
do cicada shells cling to bark and
why
do I have to eat my crusts.
and the mothers bend down to answer.

they'd all grown inside someone 'til they were
ready
to make noises and breathe and have porcelain skin and limbs
with perfect fingers.
ready
to be loved.

mine bled out of me (cells in a tiny sac leaving gently
almost as we discover them).
but then you stayed tucked inside me for months
'til I almost waddled and spent hours bent over my belly
answering your kicks, speaking softly of our imagined future.
we marvelled as your paddles turned to perfect fingers and toes
between ultrasounds.

they couldn't tell us
why
you bled out of me too. all your organs intact but
quiet.
only 19 inches long, but complete
-ly still.
my body beating with tiny contractions
like your lost
heartbeat.

and I wasn't
ready
for how much you were to be loved.

My Father's Hands
Maree Reedman

Long, tapered fingers,
like candles.
Not a musician,
though your sister
tried to teach you the piano.

A gardener
of fruit trees and roses
until you toppled over the rosemary;
the builder
of a mustard bookcase for my childhood
and my adolescent home;
a maker
of home brew
and pongy dog stew.

Your half-moons purpled
with blood as I held
your hand
while you snored,
mouth open
you always slept
easily.

My brother tried to close your lips
when you left,
off to go on that long-awaited
honeymoon with Mother,
the one you never took.

Something for Nothing
J.J. Hicks

His things came home in May. Hospital ID labels slapped onto garbage bags with finality. Indelible black dots, spewed out by a printer and processed without sympathy; no card or ribbon as a gesture of closure. Instead, brisk black knots clenched in resolution against the pain inside. She left the black bags full of smells and memories to loiter in the garage.

The cold fingers of dawn pierced through the cracks into a dad-sized hole in her life; empty days without appointments, outings and the business of caring. A worm of guilt gnawed at her relief in knowing where he was, or wasn't . . . .

'Dad's gone missing again. Is he there?'
'He's not here for the bus; we think he hitchhiked to Horsham.'
'Grandad just walked here in the heat; he's hallucinating.'
'Can you come into town? He won't get into the hospital car.'
'Nobody can find him and it's getting dark.'

His diminishing world became more baffling to him, while hers swelled like a complicated pregnancy nurtured in a barren womb. Her life took a backseat until death swooped in—unexpected and shocking.

Christmas. Time for making way for the new, to grasp at joy. With her sights set on a Lifeline shop fifty kilometres away she feigned brevity and assembled the black bags, breathing through pursed lips to avoid the smells of memories as she untied the knots. She distanced herself by creating order, and set aside shabby items for her husband to whisk away behind the scenes, like their dead family pets.

The things that were important to him made her falter: his photos and books; the bits and pieces of a life confined to a small square room for his last two years. Stacks of monogrammed hankies emerged—he'd filled his pockets with them as part of his dressing routine—and she paused to hold a watch he insisted on wearing, although he couldn't read it. He started each day fortified with this armour: ready for anything—a man in control of life's mishaps and in control of time. His wallet was sacrosanct; she half-smiled about the weird places he'd hidden it. It contained his long-expired driving licence and a stash of five-cent coins, and tucked behind a yellowed plastic window was his pride—his last shred of personal dignity: a DVA GOLD card.

Here was formal recognition—a symbol of gratitude, prised out of the system decades too late, finally granted during the year he went into care. It was something tangible to be carried with pride; proof of official thanks for his service during the War in Korea, a stab at recompense for a battler who raised a family during his hard-earned life. He felt important with this shiny gold card and boasted about receiving free health care with fringe benefits—all of them meaningless in the confines of that three-by-three room. At last he had something to show for it all. He called it 'something for nothing'.

Position Vacant—Apply Within
Jacqui Bakewell

Would you like to be my new best friend? You see, I have a vacancy. Two actually.

The vibrant, the hilarious and charming Hig has left me. The stunningly beautiful, gracious and loving Donna left also, eighteen months later. And it's left a bit of a hole in my life. You see, we'd shared rather a lot.

In our late teens we booked a cabin on Fairstar (The Fun Ship) and drank our way across the Pacific Islands. We watched the movie *Top Secret* so many times in the ship's cinema that we were able to act it out verbatim—including the dance. We spent darkened nights in the airless cabin whispering about boys and carved our names into The Animal Bar. We went snorkelling and got the fright of our lives when we followed a school of fish out past the shelf, the black ocean yawning abruptly below us.

We supported each other through broken hearts and our first forays into independence. We spent Friday nights at the Aussie Hotel singing *Livin' on a Prayer* at the top of our lungs. When Hig moved away to the coast, Donna and I would visit, spending the weekend shopping for tie-dyed clothing and catching live bands. To share the travel, I taught Donna how to drive my manual car and we would jerk along home with the gear box screeching.

In our twenties, Hig took off to Canada whilst Donna and I headed to Europe. Three weeks squashed into a double decker bus with thirty two singles from all over the world. We sunbaked topless in the French Riviera. We saw the Mona Lisa, and drank steins in the beer halls. We hired a car and motored through Britain. We saw a beautiful field of wild flowers and without saying a word I pulled over and we ran out and frolicked in them.

We returned home where adulthood awaited. I accepted a marriage proposal and Hig held my hair back as I puked everything up on my hen's night. She held my train as I walked down the aisle. Over the next twenty years we shared seven births, one miscarriage, two episodes of postpartum psychosis. One marriage ended. Another was saved.

And finally, two cancer battles. Two deaths. Two funerals. They were in their forties.

And that leaves me—with a vacancy for a best friend (or two).

But there is a problem. The bond that shared history gives you is not replaceable. The void is as wide and scary as the ocean that swallowed us off the Isle of Pines. I didn't just lose my best friends. I lost the ability to share the memories of our youth. These girls were meant to age with me, giggle with me as we fanned away hot flushes. We would 'Remember when . . . ?'

You cannot 'remember when?' Not with me. So I'll withdraw the vacancy.

But if you know the waltz from *Top Secret* I'm up for it.

Grief Riff

Mark Tredinnick

there is a landscape, veined, which only a child can see
or the child's older self, a poet . . .
—Adrienne Rich, "Dreamwood"

End of a lonely day
                    spent watching rain
Showers lift and fall,
Drafting—and erasing—landscapes
                                  across the hours.
My children are scattered like thoughts
I could not keep.
                    Night falls
On the harbour now, and I search
For a book to keep me
From my grief,

                    to find my sorrow—
And recollect my wealth—written
Out in other lives and other times and ways:

            For each of us is all of us,
                      in the end, and morning
Is only hours away.

Suddenly You Were Gone
Susan Bradley Smith

Our plans—to see the northern lights and survive
Antarctica and everything in between—were stupid.
When you told me you were dying my fists hated you
more than cancer loved the clever speed of your
blood. And I knew then what it meant to be a
world-class fool. No false Falstaff, the ways of
the vain and the boastful and the cowardly became
mine, became me. You would've been right to
repudiate me, but you didn't. You said one sentence
more—it included the phrase 'our children'—then
(perhaps you are the buffoon?) left me for good,
for the worst, before the better which you'd
promised would come.

This kingdom you have bequeathed me is all
blood oranges on hot china, and granulated salt
on grazed knees. At first. For a long time, it just
remains weather, this world of grief, mostly squeaked
cloud mass with not a human in sight. Memories
are reliable storms, and I take no shelter, I let them
age me and tell me my story, allow them to sepia
my soul. I grow foreign to my children,
until one day your son turns around to me—
he is wearing your ancient Paul Smith suit, in which
I think you married one of your wives, and your
old Joy Division Tshirt, and his own Converse—
and there you are: back from the dead. He is so, so
happy, about to go wildly dancing, with those limbs
of yours, that boy of ours. Well someone has to, I think:
be happy. And live. Like we were; we did. If I dared,
I'd ask *How are you, up there?* But I remain afraid
of rain, and unsure of my grip on honour, or answers.

Of Cold Hands
Justine Poon

A small ritual between us: my grandmother used to often tell me that her hands were cold and hold those hands out for me to see for myself. I would then hold her cold hands in mine, passing back my warmth. *Shuut-gum-doong,* cold as ice, she would say in Cantonese. When I was hot-headed or exhausted I would sit next to her as she watched TV and hold her hands against my face for comfort.

I associated gran's coolness with the sense of her diminishing flesh being replaced with the pure coldness of deep, subterranean rivers slowly and eternally moving with every drop of water filtered through countless layers of sediment above. The body's slow drag towards death is unstoppable. The blood sinks first and suddenly there's a lot less of it circulating around. Then the bones hollow out. There are successively less physiological reasons for the heart to continue, although the emotional ones remain. Finally, the breath gives out.

Before the final exhalation, this increasing submersion into timelessness seems to inspire a determination that makes up for some of the deteriorations of age. She never stopped walking up the hill behind our house; she only did it slower. She never gave up on the morning rituals of waking: putting water on the shrine and drinking tea with the cockatoos just after sunrise. Her pace was slow but steady and unfaltering. Her tiny silhouette in the distance in her beanie, black coat and pants and walking stick was unmistakable.

Her arrival always seemed so inevitable that when she stopped coming it felt like a law of nature had been upended. She was already an old woman when she took over my care as a baby and she had trained me for her death since I was old enough to understand it. Still, her constancy in my life and the certainty of mortality existed in parallel. Theory can't help you prepare for what is fundamentally unknown. The work of rebuilding, how you understand the world without someone can only begin once that person is gone.

I dream that we go to the airport and go nowhere and she says nothing. I am home and standing in the living room; she is in the corner of my eye and she says nothing. I do the ordinary things of my daily life and she is at my elbow saying nothing. I dream of showing her Kata Tjuta, or The Olgas, with snow dusting the shoulders of those great, red rocks in the desert. She says nothing.

In winter in Canberra, I hold my hand out, cupped and open until the cold air settles in it. I tell myself the stories she used to tell me. I try to remember the shape of her life, the timbre and pauses of her speech, the little rituals of her day. These are the things that leave no trace. I hold them tightly in my mind like talismans against her permanent absence.

Perseveration
Lisa Kenway

The bed has a dodgy wheel. It trundles, *ker-thump, ker-thump*, down the corridor—like a heartbeat. I hover over her. She tugs at the mask and pierces me with squally eyes.

'What happened to my baby?'

I adjust the mask with one hand and hold her gaze as we weave around the empty beds and x-ray machines. *Ker-thump, ker-thump*.

'I'm sorry. He didn't make it.'

Her brows fold inward.

'The baby died. I'm so sorry.'

She rests her head on the pillow. A single tear edges its way down her cheek. She flicks the mask off.

'Keep the mask on, you're just waking up.'

We turn into the Recovery Room and wind slowly towards the quiet corner—*ker-thump—ker-thump*—and stop. She looks up at me.

'What happened to my baby?'

'I told you, a second ago.'

She stares, blankly.

My voice cracks, distant like an echo. 'I'm so sorry. He didn't make it.'

She scrutinises the ceiling. I tilt backwards. I can't see what she sees. The nurse is fussing, applying monitors, checking her uterus is contracting, that the bleeding is minimal. All the while, she peers at the ceiling, the repeating pattern of white squares.

'What happened to my baby?'

The nurse catches my eye, her face twisted into a question mark.

'I'm so sorry . . .'

She watches me, interrogating me wordlessly. I turn heel and retrace my steps, back to the operating theatre. The monitors are mute. They've mopped the floor, turned off the oppressive radiant heater. No music, no chatter, no footsteps—suffocating silence.

'She needs to see him, hold him.'

The theatre nurse slides her body between me and the child. 'It's a coroner's case. We can't touch anything, Doctor.'

'Is it?'

'Just in case.'

I advance, inserting myself into her personal space. 'She needs to see him, to hold him.'

'She might dislodge the endotracheal tube.'

'Do you know what it feels like, to lose a child?' *To constantly resist the vortex, dragging you under?*

I grab the tube and tug. She opens her mouth and the slightest sound escapes, not a word, an exhalation.

'It fell out in transit,' I say, and she almost imperceptibly nods her head.

The baby trolley is light and careers down the corridor, whisper quiet. I swaddle him and cover the top of his head, still sticky, with the bunny rug. He's cold and tiny, floppy, inert. I lower the bundle into her arms.

'I'm so sorry.'

Her tears wash over her cheeks and spill over onto his head, connecting them like a *Bit.Fall* installation, the droplets configured precisely to create ephemeral words. I can see them, for a split second, as they fall. *Loss. Void. Love.*

She leans forward, her lips pressed gently to the soft spot over his fontanelle, then tilts her head back, examining me. Her face is blurry, my cheeks wet.

'You too?' she whispers.

I nod.

She smiles thinly, casting a net, drawing me into her realm.

'Thankyou. I'm so sorry.'

Widows
Chris Armstrong

Let the night people do their thing.
My neighbour and I are making
final arrangements for
lateness.

Across the dark lawn of his backyard
I see him on his lit veranda shuffling
those arthritic knees towards the screen
door.

He sees me across that empty space
through my window. I am washing dishes
in the fluoro lit kitchen. We see each other
see each other and
pause.

We each know about
voids.

I draw the blinds and go in
and fold the double bed in half
as I imagine night time dew
settling on your feet and I begin
writing like I never did with you
in the room.

Ketamine
Catherine Johnstone

It starts on an inward breath an explosion of brain cells and a
    parting of company
an unfettered force through his veins unfixing the fixed, subdividing
    and colliding

he has gone somewhere else already he is not mine he is in a bullfight
    with reality
and he is losing and I watch from the other side of the veil
    the vein

in his neck pounds and stretches the skin and I count the throbs
    and his breath
shakes his chest till I fear it will crack open and everything that is inside him
    will fall to the floor

I chant faithless prayers as his words roll around his mouth a stream
    of unconsciousness
what will return of him what scars have been etched into him that will haunt
    us and hunt

him down and his breathing begins to steady the prowling lion of my fear
    retreats to
the corner where I sit and wait and breathe and not breathe and count
    and he sleeps

and slips into rest and the shadows recede and he will wake to a new world.

Little Man
Camille Potgieter

I watch as the woman picks up her tiny baby and attaches him to her breast, coaxing him to suckle. She catches me looking and I quickly turn my head. There are unwritten rules in the NICU but sometimes our curiosity gets the better of us and we steal glances. The small pang of jealousy when another baby progresses to the front of the ward—the last step before going home. There are no machines in that section and the nurses are visibly more relaxed.

'How old is yours?' She asks.

'26 weeks,' I say. 'But they say he's doing well,' I quickly add when I see the shocked look on her face. She looks at his incubator and I know what she sees. At 700g he is so tiny, with so many pin-pricks from all the blood tests.

But today his body looks paler than usual. 'Maybe an infection,' a young, new nurse says flippantly. They need to draw more blood and I leave the ward because I cry when he screams. It hurts too much for both of us.

When I return they have news for me.

'We're reducing his milk intake to give him a chance to recover. We're also putting in a line, so it's easier to administer his meds.' The usually cheery head-nurse's demeanour is now brisk and she avoids too much eye contact with me.

Three weeks ago my world changed and now I know it is going to change again.

I struggle to extract milk but my tears seem to flow easily. When I return, there's an extra machine and two more nurses hovering.

The mood in the ward has changed and I can feel eyes on me.

Something happens and they lead me out of the ward. I don't argue—I'm too scared and I don't want to know the reason.

The ward becomes busy and I fade into the background and disappear.

When I go back, some time later, things are very different. I start to disinfect my hands and grab one of the crisp, clean gowns but someone gently stops me.

I am numb as I walk past the spot where the hive of activity took place a few hours ago. All the machines are now switched off and there are no nurses to be seen.

The bundle rolled up tightly inside the cot is mine.

I sit and the nurse hands him to me. I notice the tears streaming down her face as she walks away, leaving me alone with my baby. I get to hold him for the first time; to properly see his tiny face for the first time.

And he is beautiful.

And I am happy.

No more pin-pricks or noises. No more pain.

Fly free my little man.

Christian Caine Potgieter
21.05.02 – 09.06.02

Three Tiers of Grief
Margaret McBride

August 31st 1931
The Governor,
Barnardos Barkingside.

Dear Madam

    I write to you to ask you if you can give me any information concerning my youngest sister, by name, Edith Simpson, she was taken into one of your homes when she was a small child (between 5 & 7 years old) after the death of our mother. Her father's name was John T. Simpson, at the time she was living at Florentine Court, Ripon, Yorkshire. I should be very grateful to you if you could tell me if she is still in your homes or if not, where she was sent. I am in correspondence with my other two sisters and two brothers in NSW, Australia and Canada respectively and I should very much like to get in touch with little Edith. I am now happily married and have a nice little cottage of my own in a nice part of the city. I have been hoping that I might be allowed to bring Edith to live with me, as I could take good care of her now. I enclose a stamped addressed envelope for your reply and I shall be anxiously awaiting same.

Yours Faithfully,
Mrs Freda Taylor.

3rd September, 1931

Dear Madam

    I write to acknowledge, with thanks, your letter of the 31st August, and to say that your sister Edith went out to Australia with one of our parties in April 1928. Edith is extremely happy and is getting on nicely out there. The Principal of Fairbridge Pinjarra says that 'Edith has good reports all round.'

Yours truly,
Governor.

Sept, 8th 1931

Thank you very much for your reply. I have been hoping that I might be allowed to bring Edith to live with me, as I could take good care of her now and get her a good situation when she became old enough and I want to ask this one favour of you. Please don't think me selfish, but it is just the longing for my own people.

Yours Gratefully
Mrs F Taylor.

14th September, 1931

Dear Mrs Taylor
I write to acknowledge your letter of the 3rd inst., and to say that I am afraid we could not bear the expense of bringing Edith back to England, even if it were decided it would be well for her to return.

Yours truly
Governor.

****

This is the story of my mother, Edith Simpson.
Reading the letters I realized I was not only grieving for myself but for my mother, her sisters and brothers.
How could these institutions collude in such a scheme?
The 'orphans' sent to Australia were little more than child slaves—separated from family, stripped of identity and without any vestige of control over their lives.
Having uncovered the secret my mother took to the grave, these letters compounded my grief.
My mother's only sin? To be born poor.

Glazier
Moya Pacey

After he knocks off work Saturday afternoon, he rides his pushbike to Pearsons for a pane of glass, straps it to the crossbar and wheels it home along the Greenway. The weather's fine because it's summer when my brother kicks his football through our front-room window.

No-one else about. Just me standing outside on the garden path reaching my hand through the empty frame to take some putty from his hand, our fingers touching. I roll mine into a sticky pellet liking the oily smell of linseed so much I sniff and sniff. Dad's inside spreading his. Smoothing it with the knife he's borrowed from the kitchen.

Frowning and biting down on his lower lip, green eyes narrowing he holds the pane steady, arms outstretched, big hands gripping both sides, lifting and taking its weight. He stops humming. Pushes the glass gently into the frame. A bony elbow pokes out from the hole unravelling in his grey woollen jumper.

The last time I see him, he's at the station standing on the very edge of the crowd. Head bowed. Arms hanging at his side. The coach engine's revving. My knuckles rap-rapping on the window.

> *no goodbye*
> *between us*
> *rain smears the pane*

O My Sista
Kim Westwood

this ache of words
can't reach the place of you

I saw too late
—we all did:
a prism spilling out sun
        and spinning, spinning in dark . . .
then there was the cliff,
the brief sky
and the rocks

and mum getting dinner as if you hadn't done it

now there is the asking and asking
and the wanting all those strangers at your funeral away
(but) still there is no saying
that will say the thing:
how I'll miss
        I'll wish
        I'll *roar*, O my sista . . .

there is only the gone of you
flapping in my heart.

I See More Clearly Now
Patricia Green

We sat on the front veranda, a circular table between us. We had been quiet, absorbing the autumn. On the lawn, leaves from the Chinese Tallow tree worried each other. Leaning forward, she examined my face, her beautiful brown eyes now bleary with age. She placed her knobbly hand on my forearm. I loved it when she touched me with that determined familiarity, affirming our connection. I felt myself loved. Gazing at her, tears prickling, I yearned to wipe away her worries, her confusion.

For she was troubled. Each day, when I took her tablets and coffee, she was awake already and, I suspect, had been vigilant for some time. I would find her frail body rigid, arthritic fists tensed under her chin, anxiety etched on her face.

Always the anguish was about some charge to be completed—money to be found, a task not finished, a child not seen for some time. Once, she had asked if she was to go to school, worried about repercussions from nuns should she be late. That very morning, I found her lying quiescent but her face saturated with worry. 'I must get work. We need money.'

She tolerated my assurances but I believe now that her fretting was relentless.

I was the eldest of seven, she the youngest by far of a tired, ageing mother whose reservoir of love had been depleted, who was incapable of showing my mother, the child, the love she needed.

The arrival of sibling after sibling granted me status as my mother's off-sider. The arrival of sibling after sibling drained her of patience, drained her of understanding. Sometimes, I stood in loco parentis—bossy, demanding, resentful, neither adult nor child. Our relationship was fraught with conflicted love. I sought to shuck off the constraints of childhood, yet, was desperate to retain its security. She fought to understand a smart-arse kid. Years later, all rage spent, our collisions forgotten, we cared for my invalid father together.

She was a beautiful woman, slim, stylish—a woman of the war years. I loved watching her dress to go out—stockings, high heels, well-cut frocks. Never a confident woman, she dreaded saying something silly or becoming an object of ridicule. 'I'm just a dumb cluck,' she would conclude, a rueful expression shadowing her lovely face. She needed love but eschewed sentimentality. As her hearing failed, and our energetic conversations became unintelligible noise, she would retire to her room folding away the stuff of unintended exclusion without comment. Our busy lives dominated. She faded into her silence as she had as a child.

We sat. Magpies foraged. Willy Wagtails flitted. She took my wrist, an intimate gesture reserved for those she loved deeply. With a tentative smile—as if what she was about to say was foolish, fanciful—she leaned forward, her grip now a plea, and, in a voice peppered with hope, asked 'Are you my mother?'

The Funeral
Tim Slade

A seagull buries beak into feathers to sleep . . .

Now is the time to anchor
our hearts. My grandfather sails
into unchartered waters. The church ~

shiny shoes shuffle, and the logbook
turns back this old salt's pages
to the first of his life. Today,

nailed sternwards to the mast of a cray boat:
No Salesman, Religious or Otherwise . . .
We would see him last at the funeral

for his wife, Margaret. Walking down the aisle
go I. Then starboard, toward an unknown
horizon. We are now at the mercy

of the current of the church.

Figs
Jo Gardiner

Wading through drifts of dogwood leaves
she brings them in a paper bag.
I arrange them on a blue and green dish
and admire their plump forms each morning
when I come to the table for breakfast
remembering her face lined as bark
grief carved into her skin
like someone's initials onto a tree.
She brings her stories to my book-lined room
where I notice them, remark upon them
and in a long, slow conversation, we share a laugh
at her expense. Or mine.

When it's time for her to go,
she returns to the solitude of her garden
where a fig tree stands a little less laden.

Carrying On

Michael T. Schaper

Loss, Anne tells herself, can be a very selfish thing. How dare Andrew go and leave her to try and carry on like this?

She pauses. Down in the distance she can see the faint, white mark of the ocean breakers. There's a livestock truck making its way along the road, headed to her gate, as arranged.

It's an unpredictable thing, noise. Anne looks down at the yard where the cattle are waiting. Hardly a sound coming out of them. Isn't that strange? Yet she can sit up here on the porch and still hear the waves rolling in on the swell, so far away.

A perfect place to surf, Andy had often told her. Not that many places in the world where you can have a farm on the edge of a surf break. Alone. All yours.

Anne didn't surf. She'd never enjoyed the few times her husband had enticed her out into the water. The two of them alone out there. The cold, the fear when even the gentlest of breakers rolled in over them. After that, she'd been happy to leave him to it.

So she hadn't been there when he didn't come back. A fine autumn afternoon, the wind low, the sun warm and the swell the best in several days.

Not coming back: a concept she'd never thought much about, before. Someone close to you—a child, an aunt, an old school friend, a husband—walks out the door as they always do and the world seems perfectly normal, predictable. And then they vanish. Gone. No sign. No conclusion.

And then you're left alone. To carry on. Cook and sleep. Watch television, take holidays, read the newspapers. Try and run a farm.

The truck horn sounds once, twice. The driver steps out. He's got a kelpie with him, a grizzled, old dog with a mean snarl. It dashes over to the cattle pen and starts barking at the cows. Baiting them.

The cattle begin to low, just occasionally at first. Then the fear of what is about to happen takes hold and they start to moo loudly. The cows are first. Then their calves begin to join in, until all of them are braying.

'Have you made a decision?' the driver asks.

Oh, Andrew, do you realise how hard it is to be here fighting bankruptcy? Leaving me to carry on?

She shrugs disinterestedly. Calves make great veal, and prices are particularly strong at the moment. 'Sure. But I expect your cheque tomorrow.'

The young animals cry. Their mothers begin lowing frantically as the kelpie is sent in and they're separated, the calves rounded up into the truck.

Anne doesn't listen to them. She can only hear the ocean, rolling in, waiting to take someone else in due course.

Carrying on alone can be the hardest thing to do. I wouldn't wish this on anyone, she tells herself.

Hidden Grief
Vanessa Yenson

To the woman at the airport who turned and caught me looking at the back of your head, I wasn't staring. Well, I was, but not for the reason you probably thought I was. I saw the wispy blonde strands with the large patches of pink scalp underneath that seemed to reflect the light in a cruel, accentuating manner. I saw your shoulder-length effort to grow your hair and it reminded me of Jackie.

It's been almost nineteen years since we were on a Survivors' Day Retreat in Wollongong with CanTeen. Every member in remission, trying to figure out how to fit back into society: raising fears, concerns and experiences; the counsellor and the doctor trying to answer every question as best they could.

I was the oldest by far, having been diagnosed at twenty. Jackie was about fifteen but looked twelve. She agonised over when her hair would grow back properly. She'd been in remission for longer and yet my head sprouted a thick, black, unnaturally wavy regrowth. I remember feeling guilty.

For a split-second, I wondered if you were her—still looking younger than your true age. And when you turned and caught my gaze, I was remembering that I'd heard Jackie had died not long after that day. I was in the process of dredging up the memory of who told me the news when your blue eyes locked on mine. I didn't want to divert my gaze too quickly, like a guilty voyeur, so we looked at each other for a few awkward seconds.

I wanted to tell you that I understood being different, especially when it's something out of your control. I wanted to say, I relapsed, and recovery the second time was infinitely more difficult. I wanted to say that I'll never grow my hair long again because it's too thin and sparse. I'll never have children. I'll always need blood tests and checks on my bones, my skin, my breasts, my lungs, my heart.

I wanted to say that I admire you. You could challenge me with a steely gaze.

It may have been a long time since diagnosis and relapse but a very deep, inner part of me still grieves for the things that I've lost: friends, time, innocence and the security and trust in my own body.

In some strange way I also envy you. Because my story is masked by a deceiving, healthy-looking exterior. But Inside, when I take the time to reflect and remember, Inside is still raw. I see me—not quite an adult—trying to piece my way through a journey I didn't ask for and could barely comprehend. And perhaps, because of the length of time, it is a personal grief I do not feel I can share as much anymore. I should feel lucky. Eighteen years in remission. It's a milestone to be proud of and, yet, certain truths aren't any easier to face.

    A solitary grief. A lonely grief. A hidden grief.

Hanging On
Karen Whitelaw

When I wake up this morning the sun has its fingers on the closed shutter blades trying to prise them open to check I'm okay. I don't bother getting up to open them. The sun will be gone soon. If I let it in, I'll grieve the loss of its warmth later.

I put on my husband's brown-checked dressing gown. The hospital sent it home; he doesn't get up anymore. The sleeves are too long and flap about with the hands missing. I curl up in his armchair and push down the side handle so the footrest cranks up. The mechanism sticks halfway, like always, so I lift my bottom off the seat and put all my weight on my arm. Then it gives. I nearly fall over the side. If I did fall . . . when I fall, I won't want to get up.

I stare at the huge piece of flaking paint just under the picture rail. John painted the walls blue, and the rail a half-shade darker, about ten years ago. The walls are made of horsehair plaster and the rising damp on the southern side makes them crumble. Most mornings I discover fine grains of sand on the skirting board under the torn skin of paint. I noticed it first about a year ago just after John's diagnosis. The peel was small then, no bigger than a five cent piece. A shadow really, only showing up at night when we turned on the table lamp underneath. We inherited the lamp from John's mother.

The fragment has expanded and lengthened during the year. It now curls over as large as a folded A4 sheet. A couple of months ago I tried supergluing it back on the wall, but, when I eased the curling edge back over, it snapped off. I cried. But I stopped when John started crying too.

I should get up on the buffet and pull it off. One flick is all it would take. But I'd be left with this raw, gaping hole which nothing could fix, unless I got rid of the whole wall and started over again. And that's unbearable.

So each morning I come down convincing myself that the decaying wall will have miraculously healed during the night and the paint will have stitched itself back up. John will smile from his armchair, his big kind hands reaching for me from his dressing gown sleeves.

But for now, we're barely hanging on.

Roma alla John: 2011
Elizabeth Beaton

The folds of a marble dress
swirl around a gasping Madonna.
Saints' ribs rattle and dance
under the altar of the chiesa;
in cobbled streets, the sugar romance
of pistachio biscotti lures us
to windows, each wafer
anointed with cream.
Leaves fall in an orangerie
outside a crumbling moat.
The singing of Boticelli's nymphs
pursues us through alleyways
blessing our heels. We will remember them,
these days. I will feel the shade
from a cypress on Palatine Hill, years later,
the tinkle of water over the cracked lip
of a fountain in the Borghese grounds,
your hand on my shoulder
for less than a second,
all my tomorrows.

Crank
Shelley Booth

When my father almost passed away I was on the other side of the world with a man I would not marry.

'Your father has been in an accident on his motorcycle. He's had surgery. He's in a back brace. He's got a ruptured liver and they had to amputate his leg.' I release a guttural roar.

Ridiculously, I am on holiday with Michelangelo's David, yet, my mind is in the ICU. I'm travelling somewhere with dad's missing leg.

'Your dad would want you to enjoy your holiday.' I spend three weeks drinking to forget. I never forget. We break up.

Dad is, and always was, blue collar. He came from worse than nothing, yet, made his way in the world. By fourteen I was more educated than he'd ever be. By thirty I was earning more then he ever would.

When I moved out of my first cockroach-infested share house, dad set up a pulley system to lift my mattress over the first floor balcony and down onto his ute. That was nothing. When I was a child, dad would take my sister and I to a park with a giant bell at the top of a pole. It was only my dad who could reach it and let it peal across the lagoon.

They burnt his leg. My new partner, the one I will marry, has to reason with me, placate me: 'They took his leg and wrapped it nicely and placed it gently in the incinerator.'

While dad is in rehab I spend three weeks of his two-month stint visiting three times a day. Breakfast. Visit. Lunch. Visit. Dinner. Back to the hospital. I hide out in the room with dad and the other blokes until it is time to turn off the light. We are boy scouts at camp. Good night dad. Good night John. Good night Peter. Good night Bruce. Good night Bob. Good night Keith.

On my last day, I sit in my car and cry all those held in tears. *Dad can't see me like this.* I pull myself together and walk inside those pale green walls. There is dad in his wheelchair with the crank doing physio on his hand. I put my head in his lap and weep. *Something terrible has happened. I need my dad.*

'It's alright, love, it's just a leg.'

Keith, who is much younger than dad but has been bedridden for months with some strange bacteria, makes an awkward joke about my tears. I smile awkwardly back.

'Dad, do you ever hear from the blokes from rehab?' I ask during one of the many conversations post 'the accident' where I behave like nothing has changed and dad is still my dad and his leg is not a ghost that wakes me at night dragging it's foot along the floor. 'How's Keith who owned the charcoal chicken shop and spent all day in bed listening to the radio?'

'He died, love.'

Tick Yes to Donate All Organs
Rafael S. W.

My lover will one day be someone else.
A checkbox on a blue pamphlet is enough
to remind me I own nothing, and nor does he.
This skin, our treasured stamp album
of woundings. Now a passed-on passport. His grist
will be graft. I've never been in synch with his lungs
but they too will go elsewhere. Draw warm air
through strange lips. The deep sea creatures
of organs with uses I don't know, they will
be bottled briefly, or netted from his navel.
I hope I am dead before this. But he has
a six month head start. We should have
made a pact. It is not for loneliness, but rather
the fear of seeing him unzipped. Learning
it was not me who lay claim to his heart.

Miss You Much
K. Lundman Rocks

Every morning there is a transient period before dawn when first light struggles to break free of the dark. This body of mine threatens to wake. Through the fog, it threatens to remember the awful truth. My inner defences scream no as I curl up tight, pull the quilt close and bunker down into the pillow, fending off another day without you. I fall then, at last, into real slumber, free from the frantic restlessness of night. I fall deeply until I see you: you are next to me in our bed as always and we languish, cuddling together.

These are the days and nights we held each other tightly, half listening to the street below, laughing over coffee shop kisses and pistachio baklava till bursting, brimming with a joy so young and simple it needed no explanation. I was jeans and t-shirt but you were all summer dress, pale lemon and light as the air you breathed. We took the train everywhere and walked everywhere else, strutting our jackets and boots because we were king and queen, owned the city. On the beach we fed hot, salty chips to our squawking subjects and at the end of a lazy, summer day we sat in the sand with gelatos and stared mutely at the flaming ambient sky. We sweated out essays in your college room, did our laps at the pool, ate our lentils back at mine where we lived our love on a bit of ragged foam. We climbed out of your college window onto a tiny strip of stone balcony just to observe the towering jacaranda in full bloom. We sat by the bell tower, mesmerised by the Sunday carillon ringing through our souls. Oh, those late nights by the piano at *The Zambezi*, waiting until he played our Satie, just for us! And he always did, fondly watching young love riding the river of continuous becoming in the brief time allotted.

The exequies are forgotten yet I feel the touch of your unreaching hand ever stronger. In my dream you lead me up a wooden staircase, through dim corridors, wandering from room to room until we arrive at the topmost window where you draw the curtain just a little and motion me to look. I see myself, tiny, sitting far below in a park, gazing up at the unfamiliar window at which we stand. From below I see your curtain, slightly drawn.

I was there in the hospital holding your hand during the twilight. You gasped just once, lightly, in the liminal moments that separate life and death. They say you are gone but I perceive your form at the window still. I am half a world away, one foot remaining in the dawn of despair.

Chronicle
Susan Fealy

Her mother called her
Angel.

She had no time
to learn her name.

She was born
into a cage. She was

a tiny thing in a snow globe.

Light flooded her eyes,
and almost chiming toes.

Her ashes live in a white urn.

Her mother's mind
holds tiny broken wings.

A Spill of Unsaids
Libby Hart

Limb-loosener, I lose you in so many ways.

Even so, I find I'm in no hurry to carve out words,
to make a bowl with these two hands,
to reveal all of the tiny birds I whittle for you.

Instead, I've been sitting in the dark
and saying things, like *bless you,*
only half-knowing why.

And it's as if you step into the room.

I'm unable to sew up my grief.
It'd take a time machine, a pick axe,
a wrong-answer button to do so.

I think I am tattering. Torn.

Heartbare yet headstrong,
I've been opening and closing
through blue-black hours.

And wayfarer, red thread at ankle,
my every breath
blows through your hair.

This poem is about ambiguous loss. Its title is taken from 'Closer' by CD Wright (Sally Mann and CD Wright, Proud flesh, Aperture Foundations Books, New York, 2010).

Words
Nikki McWatters

We had a reticence, a shyness, between us, never speaking of tender things outright. You seemed nervous of spoken intimacy and I was timid and afraid of embarrassing you. Now that you are gone, I wish that I had pushed myself, stumbling awkwardly out of my bashfulness and told you to your face that loving you had been the most spectacular thing to ever happen to me.

Every day, since you left me all alone, I must conjure up the memories of you: those sad, dear eyes that looked at me with a bemused blend of mirth and marvel and your laugh; an explosive snort, like a repressed sneeze. Sometimes I still imagine that I hear you call my name from the other room—'Mari-A!' coming in heavy on the final syllable in an almost operatic tone. There is a bird outside the kitchen window and, when it whisks its song on the morning breeze, I swear it is you calling my name. I stop stirring my tea-cup as a film of moisture blinds me and fat splodges of tears fall to the counter. A lump of grief clogs my throat and I have to gasp hard to catch my breath.

You never took me for granted. Every trivial thing I did—the morning toast and honey, pressing your shirts, running you a bath and, in the end, massaging your hands when they got so very cold—everyday acts of mine were rewarded with such a depth of gratitude that I thought you a saint.

My life without you is stark and empty and thankless. I miss the miracle of your companionship. You were always my knight even though you wore your shining armour to protect yourself from sentimental words and never let your guard down. But not once did you forget the yellow Dahlias on our anniversary. No day went by when you did not leave me little surprising notes about the house. I worry now that you might have thought I took these things for granted but I never did. You never said the words 'I love you' but you told me in other ways a hundred times a day. Like an addict deprived of a drug, I now get the trembles when I remember you. I long for your cold hands. I wish I could still rub them warm as you sob my name 'Mari-A' in your sleep, through parchment-thin lips that had once kissed me so ardently.

I shuffle around this house we shared for seventy-two years and, as I touch each precious gift, a memory sparks. The carved cedar moose summons the smell of maple leaves in Ontario. The crystal frog—the time I hurt my ankle. You set it on my bedside table as I slept.

You let me know you loved me without words. I hope you left knowing that it was returned ten-thousand-fold. If I had you over, I would have been braver and told you the words myself.

Tinkerbell

Jessica Kennedy

Her name was Tinkerbell. Or it was to her friends, at least. To everyone else she was Kelly. Kind, sweet Kelly. She was the sort of person you could never dislike. I'll never truly understand why he did it. Why he killed her.

The day she died I wasn't even at home. I was on a plane miles away with no way of knowing what was going on. I didn't hear about it until the next day, at school, as rumours began to spread that a girl had been murdered. I figured it wasn't anyone I knew. But whispers began. Whispers that uttered her name. My friend. It seemed too horrific to believe at first, until I saw them. The girls crying, their faces twisted with distress. My stomach dropped and I began to feel the first inkling of panic rise in my throat. Could it be her? It didn't take long for the whole school to know what was going on. Everyone was more subdued than usual, those who didn't know her eyeing the rest of us with curious and concerned expressions. They were caught up in the moment. But not feeling the hurt.

As the day went on and I learnt more about what had happened, I felt myself wracked with guilt. I felt as if I had let her down. Maybe there were signs, I told myself. Maybe I should have noticed that something was wrong. No-one did though. We were all oblivious, caught in our own life dramas, ignoring the world around us in the hope that it wouldn't hurt us. Isn't that what everyone does?

The school was in mourning for the whole week. Nobody was reprimanded for skipping class and everyone was encouraged to visit the counsellor if they were struggling. I wanted to yell at them that we were all struggling, that none of us could truly understand what was going on. Why this had happened. How do you deal with it? We were barely out of childhood, our minds still clinging onto the false hope that nothing bad would ever happen to those we loved. A gun and a stepfather took away that illusion. A twin brother with no sister and no mother.

Sometimes I picture it when I think of her. The gun, her beautiful face, the sound of her heart beating frantically to keep her afloat. I can almost feel her fear, the fear of a young girl dying. Did she die before her mother? Did she feel pain? Sometimes it hurts too much, picturing her face, but I feel like I must. I couldn't bear to have her memory fade from existence. It's my responsibility to remember her. We owe her that.

When I think of her now, almost ten years on, it still makes my heart ache. I have joy, sorrow, success and failure. But they are mine and I live them. All this was taken from her. And it still hurts.

Mother as an Art Book
Julie Watts

mother, I want to open you
like an art book

read all your italics
run my finger along your

bending forms
those watermarks, their

riots and their stillness
mother, I want to open you

like an art book
hold in present time

all your paragraphs
sing them to myself

so I remember
all that beauty gone –

your vanished sentences
your Rembrandt light

and Pollock mess
lift of lip and your unclaimed

eye
mother, I want to keep you

like an art book
place tissue paper between

your vibrancy and wit
and all your quick, Zen lines.

Saving Sebastian
Rose van Son

Sebastian is getting dressed: his black jacket, his silk shirt. Around his neck a medallion shows off brassy-gold. A black shadow draws his chin. He wears no shoes. On the day Sebastian was born his father collected red chilli-peppers from the garden, red-bellied tomatoes, artichokes, green and yellow beans, and garlic heads bigger and sweeter than oranges.

Today Sebastian wears a garlic braid. His mother drapes it loosely around his neck. His sister, Seloise, holds a basket brimmed with emerald-green broccoli, celery fronds and crisp cabbage leaves. She watches as her mother ties the braid around his neck. Sebastian's father waits outside. He fingers the sun-dried tomatoes drying on the window-sill; chews a nasturtium flower.

Last winter, says his mother, good rain trickled the roots of plants, the sun beamed, the vegetables grew so juicy and tender that neighbours begged for just a small taste. She is glad she kept some back, for Sebastian, for his special day.

Champagne and wafers, chocolate and vanilla, fill the room. Sebastian's friends come to see him in his best clothes. Not wanting to appear rude or to offend, they take handfuls of wafers, smile politely and excuse themselves as they take another, nod to his grandmother, dressed, as always, in her black stockings, black dress; black and white spotted scarf ballooned in a bow under her chin. She nods in return; lights the candles. Under her arm she carries a black rooster and speckled pigeon for later, for stock. There are many to feed.

A young man appears at the door.

'We must go,' he says. 'Are you ready?'

Twelve eyes turn toward Sebastian. Seloise strokes his brow; kisses his painted lips. His mother buries her face in his jacket. They watch him leave, decorated with woven garlic heads, red-chilli peppers and a few nasturtium leaves. As his open coffin is lifted to the sun, the mourners close their eyes. He wears no shoes.

The Weight of Words
Julia Doig

Tragedy. An audacious attempt to frame our grief. I'd so often thought back to that day. When they carried him out. How I saw him. Laying there. Weak. Vulnerable. Tan turned porcelain. I remember it so clearly. I was angry. Angrier than I'd ever been before. There were no handles on body bags. No handles. How were they going to carry him? Carrying a garbage bag is more practical.

He would always tell me in his firm but slightly condescending tone, 'Don't try to understand everything. You can't help everyone. Just let it be.' I could never comprehend what he meant. It was so close minded yet overly optimistic. If everything happens for a reason then please give me one. I needed a reason for this because it made no sense. A loss of life, it couldn't just be as simple as that.

Everyone had sent letters and flowers expressing their deepest condolences and philosophical thoughts on grief and tragedy. As if a bouquet of flowers would resurrect a corpse. As if a stolen affirmation decorating a $4 hallmark card could ease the pain. I had heard the word tragedy so many times paired with so many different adjectives. Terrible, dreadful, horrific, shocking. The list goes on. And I didn't understand. A seven-letter word. Three syllables spoken to describe death. It wasn't a tragedy because a single word does not account for what happened to him.

Others would skip the formalities and carelessly ask the tough questions. The 'how' questions. But it didn't matter. He was still gone and nothing was going to bring him back. And soon they were gone too. Days turned into weeks and weeks to months. I never stopped feeling the way I felt but they stopped apologising for it.

He was lifeless in a pool of his own blood. That's not a tragedy. I'm expected to believe that it's as simple as a slip between conscious and unconscious, life and death. That his systems just stopped. That he ceased to exist. I didn't understand how his once living, breathing and vibrant body could effortlessly stop working. This wasn't tragedy. This was an annihilation.

People would ask me how I felt as though there was a simple answer. I was suffocating. I felt like I was constantly driving in the rain, alone in a car. The windscreen wipers were on but no matter how fast they pushed, I still couldn't see clearly. And no one else knew. They didn't know how I felt because they weren't in that car. They could see ahead but I couldn't, despite the endless rain being wiped away and puddled down. And even if the rain took a second to stop, the glass would fog in the aftermath and the view ahead would be slightly clearer but still hazy. Every day I was alone in this car during a storm. But there was no painless way to say this.

'Fine. I'm doing better,' I would lie, because it's easier that way.

Eschatology
Sarah Sasson

In the end we tried but we couldn't save it. In the end your hair was white, your teeth fell out but it was still you. In the end everything was too warm. In the end you filled a sports bag with clothes, took your razor from the bathroom and left. In the end we put the ashes under a magnolia tree. In the end we could no longer evolve. In the end we were the only animals on earth. In the end there was one country but not enough food. In the end there were no rainforests. In the end I moved back home. In the end I made you breakfast in the morning and bathed you at night. In the end we read backwards in Hebrew. In the end time sped up. In the end you married another woman. In the end things that were solid became smoke. In the end all you would eat was chicken soup. In the end my cat crawled under the house. In the end there were no more intentions and none of them were good. In the end we were our own undoing. In the end there were too many guns. In the end there was nothing to do but wait. In the end I felt strangely calm. In the end we all went to where we believed. In the end I loved you more than I hated you. In the end it was better than expected. In the end you said you had to let me go. In the end there were so many things to tell you.

Undo Her Fingers
Annie Riley

The bed is cold. The room is white and clean. Filled with metal instruments that look hard and sharp, ready to slice soft flesh. I am captive. The nurses hold my legs up. They hold me down. They have broken me wide open. The doctor grins. They touch me without asking. They give me instructions, all with their chilling plastic hands inside of me. Deep inside where I am warm. I tell myself to get a grip. This thing inside me moves, it screams to come out. It wrenches my body in four directions. I am drummed and used. I leave my body. I am above, watching on, unhelping like the moon.

They bring her to me. I hold on. What did my fingers do before they held her head up? How did my body sit before it rocked her? Where did this love go that pours from me now? Her mouth is soft, she is plump and ripened. I kiss her eyelids gently. They flutter like butterfly wings. Kiss her head, kiss her mouth, kiss her cheek. Her fingers and toes. She is pink and beautiful. She is looking at me. She looks only at me.

I see her in my sleep. I hear her, she is howling. Down a long bright corridor. Her cries cut through the glass that separates us. She is trying to tell me something. I do not understand. It cannot be good. I am terrible. There's a tiny heart inside her somewhere. Pumping my blood through her limbs, her eyes search around the room for my arms. Her crying scratches at my mind until I am woken

My eyes peel open. I am so tired, I can barely wake. Two nurses look down on me. They are not joyous. They tell me the thing I cannot bare to hear. They tell me the worst thing I have ever heard in my life. They bring her to me. She does not move now. Her mouth is blue. She is so little. She is still and peaceful. Sometimes this happens, they say. They give me back my empty suitcase. I gave life. I created a corpse. My heart's a bleeding red rose, the prickly stem punctures my chest. The rain outside pummels, it is furious at me. The nurse reaches out to take her away. I undo her fingers from mine, like unwrapping a bandage. I let go.

I walk onto the college lawn. The flowers are in bloom, sweltering in the heat. Pollen sprinkles through the air. A new year. A guy walks by, his arms around the shoulders of a girl, her hair long and blonde to her waist. They pass by. I am an island. I dreamt of her last night. I pushed her off to sea in a little basket. It was only a dream. I push her off now. I let her go.

Inner City Living
Wendy McLean

Rosa's back fence faced my front door. Inner city living. We lived like that for ten years. She was old and I was young, fresh out of uni. We met through her blind and arthritic dog, Action. We laughed together at the irony.

Almost daily we would see each other, walk together.
    We would stand and talk until we had finished, time not a factor. She would look directly into my eyes and talk of her life, while holding my hand. She had survived the war. Her family was murdered. She came to Australia. She lost a husband, had four children. A part of her neighbourhood. Her friends used to live in my house, it was their house and now it is mine. Her community would wake each other anytime of the night, and that was okay. They needed each other. They all came from a time and place where that was how it needed to be, everyone was hurt. It was lost now. Gone. A whole world extinct. We would hug, hold hands and let our eyes well up.
    Action died. I saw her less. Sometimes she knocked on my door, I was always so happy to see her. I was busy having babies. Holding me tight she would instruct me to enjoy it, it is the happiest time of your life she would say. The time where you have everything and are blind to it. I looked into my babies' eyes and held on tight. One day I would be Rosa and I cried. For her, for me, for the horror of living in a lost world. The unspoken price we pay for living a long life.
    Every time I saw her she was sadder. More friends passing, never to be seen again. She said she was too old for a puppy but she got herself busy, Rosa was a fighter. New friends every Thursday morning at the local community centre. She said it was never the same, but it helped.

I stepped onto my street, I saw her two sons. I knew Rosa was gone. Standing still, child on hip, they saw me. They came, they talked. Yes, she had died. Her funeral is tomorrow. Please come. I did. I went and listened to strangers talking about her life. I sat tight in my seat. Determined to not give in to the pain. I lost.

Old Habits
Melissa Willings

Old habits are hard to break. Marriage is really just a collection of habits. Habits you like. Habits you hate. Routines. Frustrations. Suddenly, they're all gone. There is a void.

I catch myself. from time to time, looking up from the newspaper at breakfast, about to ask for an opinion or share a joke. I see the empty chair and the sharp stab of grief is renewed.

Even the annoyances are missed. The little offences you complained endlessly about seem more endearing once lost.

It's not the birthday days or anniversaries that are hard, they pass with a fond reminiscence. It is the odd moments when you slip back into old habits. I'll be in the hardware store and turn to the empty space next to me to ask the name of the item. When I'm cooking dinner, occasionally, without thinking, I reach for my phone to text to ask what time he'll be home, the blank screen reminding me there's no one to text. Once I accidently bought the bread he liked, that I don't eat. The devastation renewed afresh when I threw it in the bin. The loss of those routines is the most painful.

I cry sometimes at night when I can't sleep and it occurs to me I'm waiting for the key in the lock. Waiting to hear footsteps that will never resound up our hallway again. My hallway now. Mine alone.

Those are the moments that I grieve.

I grieve a million, tiny, insignificant rituals and habits that now take on a meaning that they never had in life. Once inconsequential and now seen as the precious beauty of life, our life together, to be treasured in memory only, now lost forever.

Old habits are so very hard to break.

Dear Grief,

You undo us quietly now,
slip a narrow finger through our seams
to tease stitches we carefully laid,

but you came at first unrelenting,
a tide wrenching, roaring in from every shore.
You were the flooding darkness
and we saw no higher ground;
we may have drowned in the loss of our child
had we not begun building weirs.

You then crept in, wily, while we slept
to perch like a dark bird on our chests,
claws at each heart, cawing us into waking

so we learned to use light to barricade the windows,
buried the betrayal of flowers in the heap
at the bottom of the yard and put lead
to the new pages of our narratives.
These days, grief, you undo us quietly
because we know now how death comes,
and we know how you find us.

Kristen Roberts

Notes on the disappearance of a friend

Charlotte Guest

In time, it becomes bearable:
this is the most unbearable part.

Time pushes you along like a celestial wind;

or you sit with your knees under your chin
in a boat on an indigo sea.

Everything is upside down,
like sunlight coming through floorboards,

like lowering food to your mouth.

Silver memories – accents on a calm harbour –
are too bright to look at.

Virga
David Francis

I have read that mourning, by its gradual
toil, its indescribable burden,
slowly erases pain. I do not believe,
cannot believe,
that proposition. For me, time only dilutes
the emotion of loss, does not erase it.
I no longer weep
for what is motionless,
for what is held in distant murmurs
beyond the hills of storms.
What I have lost is not
the abundance of a past,
but a being.
Not a being, a quality of being.
Not the indispensable
but the irreplaceable, the plays of sunlight,
individual flames
of a fire.
What remains
is absolute, unqualifiable,
rods of rain or ice that
trail from clouds,
never reach the ground,
never heal the breach between
heaven and earth, never find the edge
of certainty.

Bright Shadow
Fiona Abbey

Poltergeists, they say, are attracted to the presence of children. Grief, I think, is not. While it found many ways to pick me up and throw me to the ground, winding me and leaving me bloodied, my grandsons unwittingly helped me gather gritty pebbles of defiance to throw back in its face.

Young, seemingly unscathed and curious, they were intent on exploring the new world we had been catapulted into. We set off, leaving grief and its dragons sitting on the fence spluttering in shades of grey and smoky gloom while we threw ourselves into salty oceans and turquoise swimming pools. We shrieked and somersaulted and did hand stands, ducked under waves and shot through them to the other side, the water joining with my hands to help me lift my smallest, least seaworthy body high in the air until he too discovered he could float and sink and come up laughing.

We licked ice cream and admired our sticky smiles; fought with seagulls over hot chips in crinkled paper; swung higher and higher on swings and twirled faster and faster on giddy play equipment. At night we remade the ocean, squirting blue and green bubbles into baths too full with water. My boys would emerge onto the sodden floor, fluffy knights in soapy armour, ready to do battle with the bubble monster which emerged through the floor drain as it struggled to cope with so much fun. After stories with silly voices and stroking small noses and cheeks into a safe, deep sleep, I could look at grief squarely and say that I was too tired for despair. Grief, unimpressed with my flagrant disregard for battle plans, would stomp off in search of other short term prey, leaving me in the lamplight to feel the quiet and the difference in my slow and stumbling way.

Slowly, brick by brick, giggle by giggle, new memory by new memory, I built our defence against grief and its marauding, barbarian behaviour. A small puppy joined our ragged regiment—come to make us laugh and lick us out of dark corners. She was soon joined by two delinquent cats, rescued from certain extinction, and come to use our timber floors for rugby matches. Our kitchen table became a scattering of coloured pencils, Lego bricks and glossy brochures, promises of a future that we could build and inhabit and make our own.

And then one day, without fanfare or warning, grief snuck away, retreating into its shadows, taking with it nothing of value and leaving nothing of value behind.

My pleasure now is to take a coffee, a book and a moment out onto the ramparts of my new and very different life, which is developing its own familiar creaks and favourite corners. At times it is too small and can stub my toes or graze my soul but for the most part, after a squirm and a wriggle, I can make it fit just fine.

All Souls Are Sleeping
Danaë Killian

All souls are sleeping,
drowning, waking;
I cannot hold onto my soul
beneath my ribs.

China lies under water;
your face is wet and black
and full of dreaming, sinking
stars.

My right foot is cold
and lame like the mountain
holding itself still
under the cold flood.

But I cannot hold onto my soul
beneath my ribs: my soul flows
out
into the night.

It flows out into the wet
night of your starfilled face
faraway
in the Phoenix Hills

flowing
over me;
it flows out into the night where all souls sleep
and drown, sink and wake

crippled and cold, obstructed.
I lie undreaming and unmoving on my bed of straw.

My lungs are empty;
my hands hold still—
wordlessly, the chimney
smokes above my head, while

China lies,
mountainous,
under many valleys of soulfilled and starfilled black
water.

Lament after *I Ching* hexagram 39: *water above, mountain below* – Jian

A Bridge too Far
Tracey Edstein

My father died at midnight on a Thursday evening. It was, as seems often to be so, sudden-at-the-end, but, since the bone cancer diagnosis some five months earlier, it had been anticipated. As he became weaker and less able to enjoy any aspect of what had been a rich and engaged life, his to-do list changed.

Much to my mother's chagrin, he insisted on 'getting things in order'—although it is doubtful that anything was, or had ever been, out of order.

He reinforced things we, his wife of fifty years and three daughters, had always known. The big one, destined to be ignored—more chagrin for Mum—was 'You know I don't want anyone speaking at the funeral.'

Dad was, at the end, longing for death and all too aware that life had bestowed all its gifts, and then some.

Only my younger sister, who lived nearest to the hospice, was with him when he died, although I had left him only hours earlier. Because it was the middle of the night we were told that a doctor would come from the hospital but it might be a few hours. We elected to sit with Dad and while it must have been 5am when the young doctor arrived, full of care and apologies, it didn't seem so long.

While ever we sat with Dad he would remain with us. There was no hurrying us on for the next hapless patient to take his place. Some family members cut locks of his beautiful silver hair, which never lost its lustre, even as his life ebbed away.

Once we left the room which had barely been Dad's for twelve hours, such are the challenges of being admitted to a hospice, we would have to face the fact that life went on around us.

I had driven Mum from the town where she and Dad had made their home for exactly fifty years. When I bought my own home it wasn't far away. One consequence of this was that to be 'out'—shopping, at the parish church, walking the streets Dad had made his own—was to be asked how Dad was. I was grateful to have our family's reality acknowledged and, most of the time, I could answer honestly without losing it.

As I drove Mum home to an empty house, her mind was reeling with a 'to do' list. She rehearsed the list of those who needed to hear that Dad had died directly from her, most importantly his sister and brother. We discussed what was the earliest we could reasonably phone the parish priest, in order to begin making funeral arrangements.

As we crossed Hexham Bridge on that late September morning, the sun was rising, brilliantly and beautifully. I cross that bridge almost daily, and, most of the time, it's not significant. But, every so often, that first sunrise Dad didn't witness comes back to me in a rush. And I lose it still.

The Secret Dreams of Agistment Cattle
Philip Neilsen

At dawn currawongs industrial in their insistence.
August fog rises off the Clarence
and we see the great heads come through,
drifting behind the angophoras.

Before we piled a bush rock border
under our cabin, with a sheet of corrugated iron,
they would come in to sleep there,
holding our floor up with their breath.

Anna had a dream that they placed
their shoulders to each of the corner posts
and with eyes closed in concentration
brought down the cabin.

She also dreamed about her dead sister,
the artist, who sketched the cattle
that time she visited, and pinned a charcoal picture
of the restless herd to our wall.

The farmer stopped paying for agistment.
Then he snipped through the wires on our east fence
so his cattle came back anyway. We heard they laughed
about us, the tree huggers, in the Woodenbong pub.

Anna said the cattle had given her the bad dreams.
On her own she walked back to Sullivan's with seven
Herefords and returned in quarter-moon dark, singing,
grumbling because we hadn't cut more firewood.

In the morning she burned the leftover
funeral orders of service and the curled sketch
of cattle crossing near Tooloom Creek,
threw away the last of her medication.

The Sword

Kim Gunst

Grief is anger. Hard, cold, useless anger that sticks in your throat and makes your words so hard and sharp that they cut. Even the simple ones, the easy ones, flickering out like knives drawing blood wherever they land. Anger that is hopeless frustration, desperation and wailing, wandering, searching. Searching for a comfort for answers . . . . Or just for a moment's peace from the relentless knowledge of how small and human you really are.

Grief is cold and twisted. It strips you down to bare parts, nothing spare, the minimum required for breath and for action and momentum. Life's inexorable flow only encourages grief to cut more from you as if moving through the flow of life can only be done as the dark pieces strip away. Not that you care at all when your heart is cold and your soul is enraged.

Grief is power. Grief comes on and on pounding like a storm until you realize—it's not going to stop. Not the old ones that still hurt nor the ones to come that make you fear and hide. Grief makes you decide what you can accept and what you will not. Grief turns you into a mighty sword that cuts away all obstacles that interfere with joy. A sword that removes diseased thoughts and miserable actions. Grief becomes emblazoned when you realise it won't stop coming. But you are a warrior now and you have been given your sword.

Through the Glucose
Bee Penrose

The sea of pain she's in is thick, like glucose. I'm looking at her through a syrup of fear, her breath staggered, movement restricted, her reason distorted. Seeing Bianca failing to find god, capital g, big old h, makes me ashamed. She always knew my god was a false one. Notions of 'father', heavenly or otherwise, spark a flurry of fury which compounds the stickiness of her sea. Panic to extract herself from the dense liquid, contorts and constricts Bianca's ordinarily bright expression to a dim trickle and smothers her sense of humour. Despite being aflame with past tortures, present illness and encompassing fatigue, she battles against the glucose, towards an invisible surface. Bianca's exertion to avoid this grief, pulls her deeper than the initial plunge of unforeseen anguish provoked by the news of my death.

It wasn't unexpected, more merciful to lose my whole life in a heartbeat, than secede from it one leg at a time. The news came as pneumonia was taking hold of my daughter; as Bianca was processing our last conversation. We had a difficult relationship, we didn't speak often; the last time we did speak, took Bianca a bottle of whiskey and a month of meditation. I desperately needed Bianca to approve of me and ignore her grievances. Bianca needed me to acknowledge how I bequeathed many of those grievances to her before she could talk. I couldn't face it. I couldn't summon the courage. Bianca had to summon something special to be able to talk to me that night, without mentioning the 'patriarchal pachyderm' as she calls it, that always accompanies me and her into a room. I was elated to see my daughter, outside of the glucose, one last time. Bianca couldn't share my glee in superficiality and ignorance—she's wise, she knew it was killing me. I wish I could've known the difference between blame and responsibility, before I died. Bianca wishes I had never married a paedophile.

Underneath decades of powdered skin, the landfill of my lifetime's accumulation spoke, permeating the sickly ocean, to validate Bianca's memories. Sifting through hoarded artifacts of abuse and poverty, confirmed her courage, and consolidated her conviction. Learning my part in creating her experience of swimming in emotional concrete was torture. Wading through the relics of my woeful past, Bianca took much more than she would keep. Meticulously assembling clues, composing an accurate picture of us, she knew that collecting my things was the key to letting go. Forgiveness had long been Bianca's goal when it came to me, but a wall of fire, her justified rage, prevented her from showing it. After losing her to adulthood, I had no idea of how hard she had been working to forgive me. Her effort to traverse that blaze was bigger than anything I ever gestured to her. Brave, clever, beautiful Bianca bathed in the cement of my legacy, endured tsunamis of tears, flooded by grief's glucose, transformed those flames to fuel a loving, liberated ascent.

Overcoming Hurdles
Jacqueline Becker

That overwhelming anguish I felt so many years ago hit me again in the chest recently. It took me right back to that awful time twenty-three years ago. How I got through those early years is still a mystery to me. There have been so many hurdles. One being the question of how many children I had. Saying 'none' would have been an injustice to my son. I had a child for almost seventeen years and, in an instant, I was childless. I loved being a mother and to have that suddenly taken away from me was unbearable. Three years later I decided to reinvest in life by having more children. Nowadays I am comfortable saying I have two teenagers and one who died tragically years ago. We all have choices to make in life. Mine was to have more children at the age of forty and forty-two.

Over the years I have encouraged others, wherever possible, to have more than one child. I'm glad I did as having my pigeon pair has been my lifesaver. I smile when I think back to the birth of my daughter: how surprised I had been expecting it to be a boy again. How silly of me, especially with today's modern technology, where one can so easily find out the gender of the unborn baby. So tears it was but not for long. Looking back, it was the best thing that happened to me as I could not compare her with her deceased brother. She was a constant joy and somehow eased the pain. Having another child or children can never replace the one that has died but it does help. I know of others in similar situations but who could not conceive and who have become bitter with age. The old adage 'You can either become better or bitter' comes to mind.

The next hurdle was his 21st birthday. Another blur. On birthdays and anniversaries, I stayed home and planted a rosebush in his memory. How valuable the advice given at the time: to not make any major changes for a while. At first all I wanted was to get away from that house, that pain. Whilst away, I craved to be back in his room! I heard of people selling their homes and then sitting outside longing to be back inside.

Another hurdle was the tenth year of his passing. The build up to the day was worse than the day itself. The equator feeling was another huge hurdle for me: Brendan was now longer dead than alive.

I was asked by U3A recently to give a talk about the wonderful support group that helped me. I had been excited to share this with others but on the day I was a total mess as my father had just died. His death brought back all those emotions of losing my son, so, it does not matter how long the grief is, it's always there.

Tucked away yet always present.

Not Grief

Viktoria Rother

How can I grieve for someone I'm not sure I loved?

How can I mourn a parent whose mind was already dead?

Who couldn't remember my mother or my sister?

Who saw only his own dead?

Who saw in my sister, in my mother, his mother as she was during The War?

Who was unable to speak during his final months?

Who spent most of his time asleep, waiting to die?

Who did not know me, did not see me, but clutched my hand as I sat next to him, holding his?

Who was so emaciated that my elderly mother and I could lift him from his chair?

My magnificent, imposing, intelligent, visionary, charismatic, angry, damaged, tall, dark, handsome father: just skin stretched over his bones like the finest of plastic film. Nothing else. Lost in his memories, lost in his past; lost once more in the hell that is the lot of a child refugee. Unable to share with us, his only family—a wife and two daughters—the truth about his past. Because a brain eaten by cancer has no memory, cannot speak, is not conscious. It is, in truth, a brain that is already dead.

Did I weep for him? No.

Do I miss him? No.

I asked only that I be permitted to see him in his coffin. I kissed his forehead. I was so warm, alive; he was not. The day was hot; he was not. He was my father and yet he was not. How could this frigid, dry flesh be my father? My father was all passion, all rage, all alive. Always. This in that coffin was not him. Dead flesh; so dry; so unhuman.

Yes, he was dead.

And I? I did not grieve.

I still do not grieve.

Indian Summer
Ross Gillett

1

I wanted a wigwam
My Father Christmas father
found me one.

He pitched it at night,
pushing pegs
into the dark grass,

lacing the flap shut.
He made my dream tent
tight as a drum.

2

From inside,
the red stencilled chief
glowed on the calico.

He kept me company,
but I saw the gaps
holding him together.

The feathers he wore
were flames
staying away from him.

3

I loved the slant
of my father's shadow
sloping over the walls

as he prowled around me.
He was my enemy tribe.
Caught,

he crept backwards,
his weightless shape
sliding off.

4

I didn't come out.
He couldn't fit in,
but he bent double

to talk treaties,
his face filling the entrance
upside down.

He spoke with a stern grunt.
He knew
the no smiling rule.

5

There were days
when the wind pulled
at my thin home

and I sat in a flapping
that loosened everything.
In winter, it lived

lightly under my bed,
a big rag
waiting for summer.

6

I think of that frail
shelter, the door
no one could knock on,

with the faded chief
and, I imagine,
the faint shape

of my father's shadow.
All folded up
and put away for ever.

www.ingramcontent.com/pod-product-compliance
Lightning Source LLC
Chambersburg PA
CBHW070603010526
44118CB00012B/1435